콰트로 Quattro Grammar

Start

Quattro Grammar Start

출판일 | 1판 1쇄 발행 2014년 1월 10일

지은이 | 김정주, Peggy Anderson
펴낸이 | 강기철
책임편집 | 박혜선
영문교열 | 최용재, 하응천, 양경식, 임현주, 박송현,
              Anne Taylor, Brian Williams
디자인 | 성윤지, 이세래나, 최연수
일러스트 | Deborah Gross, John Carrozza
펴낸곳 | (주)컴퍼스미디어
등록번호 | 제22-2943호
등록일자 | 2006년 6월 16일
주소 | 서울특별시 서초구 서초2동 1360-31 정진빌딩 3층
전화 | (02)3471- 0096
홈페이지 | http://www.compasspub.com

ISBN | 978-89-6697-651-5

Photo credits
All photos and images © Shutterstock, Inc.

Quattro Grammar 시리즈는

Quattro Grammar는 영어교육의 글로벌 기준 컴퍼스미디어의 자기주도형 영어 문법 학습 시리즈입니다.

✎ **중학교 개정교과서 문법 완성**
현재 전국의 중학교에서 사용하는 주요 영어 교과서의 핵심 문법 사항 및 어휘를 모두 수록하여 내신 연계성을 강화하였습니다.

✎ **내신 서술형 완벽 대비**
현재 전국의 중학교에서 시행되는 중간 · 기말고사 문제를 철저하게 분석하여 내신 지필고사를 완벽히 대비할 수 있도록 하였으며, 특히 점차 비중이 높아지고 있는 서술형 영작 문제 공략에 역점을 두었습니다.

✎ **생생한 예문**
참신하고 생동감 있는 예문을 제시하여, 따분한 문법 공부 대신 구체적인 상황을 떠올리며 문법을 이해하고 연습하도록 하였습니다.

✎ **기초부터 심화까지 나선형 문법 학습**
〈문법 요점 정리 — Pop Quiz — Grammar Practice — 내신 대비 실전문제〉까지 4단계 점진적 학습을 〈Start → Jump → Master〉 3권 시리즈를 통해 나선형으로 반복 수행하게 함으로써 영문법의 기본적인 원리부터 까다로운 뉘앙스의 차이까지 체계적으로 실력을 다지도록 하였습니다.
또한 Mobile Vocabulary App을 통한 부가적인 어휘 학습으로 기초 영어 실력을 향상시키도록 하였습니다.

특히 Quattro Grammar 시리즈는 다독과 스피킹 중심의 어학원 영어 교육 프로그램에 익숙한 학생들이 학교 내신 및 입시에 순조롭게 적응하는 데 더할 나위 없이 좋은 길잡이가 될 것입니다.

컴퍼스미디어 영어교육연구소

Table of Contents

이 책의 구성과 특징

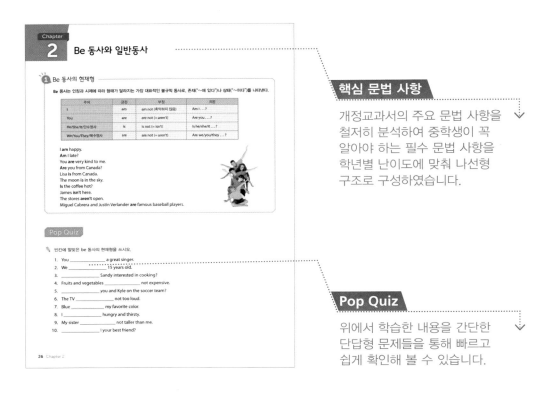

핵심 문법 사항

개정교과서의 주요 문법 사항을 철저히 분석하여 중학생이 꼭 알아야 하는 필수 문법 사항을 학년별 난이도에 맞춰 나선형 구조로 구성하였습니다.

Pop Quiz

위에서 학습한 내용을 간단한 단답형 문제들을 통해 빠르고 쉽게 확인해 볼 수 있습니다.

Grammar Practice

앞에서 학습한 핵심 문법 사항을 쓰기 위주의 연습문제를 통해 중간 점검합니다. 생생한 예문을 통해 실생활에 유용한 영어 표현도 습득할 수 있습니다. 또한 다양한 쓰기 문제 유형을 통해 내신 서술형 문제에 대비할 수 있습니다.

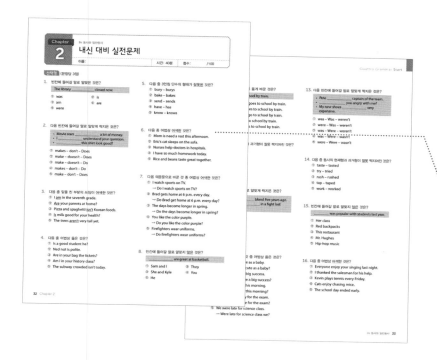

내신 대비 실전 문제

해당 챕터의 문법 요점을 실제
학교 중간 · 기말고사 문제
유형에 맞춰 연습할 수 있습니다.
실제 시험과 최대한 유사하게
구성하였습니다.

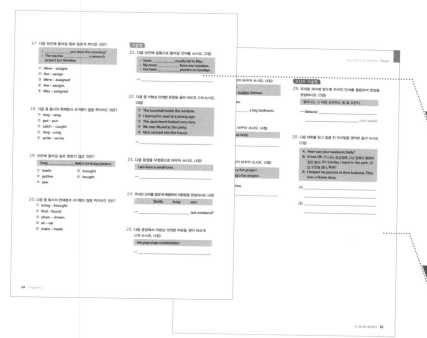

서술형

점차 비중이 높아지고 있는
내신 서술형 유형을 연습할
수 있습니다. 서술형 문제에도
난이도를 달리하여 더욱
체계적으로 학습할 수 있도록
하였습니다.

고난도 서술형

고난도 서술형은 논술형 문제
유형을 응용하여 고득점까지
완벽히 대비할 수 있도록
하였습니다.

Quattro Grammar Jump

Quattro Grammar Master

Chapter

1

Quattro
Grammar
Start

문장의 종류와 문장 5형식

문장의 종류와 문장 5형식

1 문장이란 무엇인가?

문장이란 하나 이상의 단어로 완결된 생각이나 느낌을 나타내는 글의 단위를 말한다.
영어 문장은 대문자로 시작하여 마침표, 물음표, 또는 느낌표로 끝난다.

This sentence a is. (문장 X)   → This is a sentence. (문장 O)
this is not a sentence (문장 X)   → This is not a sentence. (문장 O)
is This a sentence? (문장 X)   → Is this a sentence? (문장 O)

Pop Quiz

A. 다음 중 문장에 해당되는 것에는 O, 문장에 해당되지 <u>않는</u> 것에는 X를 쓰시오.

1. you will fall in love.　　　　　　　　　　　　　(　　)
2. Is Wendy scared?　　　　　　　　　　　　　(　　)
3. Run!　　　　　　　　　　　　　　　　　　　(　　)
4. MERRY CHRISTMAS　　　　　　　　　　　　(　　)
5. Greg wrote an email.　　　　　　　　　　　　(　　)
6. Turned a loaf into of bread she suddenly.　　　(　　)
7. Mad About You　　　　　　　　　　　　　　(　　)

B. 다음 중 완성된 문장이 들어 있는 그림의 번호와 문장을 밑줄에 쓰시오.

1.

2.

3.

4.

2 문장의 종류

1 평서문: 생각을 단순하게 전달하는 문장으로, 주어로 시작하여 마침표로 끝난다.
주어의 인칭과 수에 따라, 문장의 시제에 따라 동사의 형태가 달라진다.

주어	일반동사	Be 동사
긍정문 (현재형)	I/You/They **like** pizza. He/She **likes** pizza.	I **am** hungry. You/They **are** hungry. He/She **is** hungry.
부정문 (현재형)	I/You/They **do not** like pizza. (= **don't**) He/She **does not** like pizza. (= **doesn't**)	I **am not** hungry. You/They **are not** hungry. (= **aren't**) He/She **is not** hungry. (= **isn't**)
긍정문 (과거형)	I/You/He/She/They **liked** pizza.	I/He/She **was** hungry. You/They **were** hungry.
부정문 (과거형)	I/You/He/She/They **did not** like pizza. (= **didn't**)	I/He/She **was not** hungry. (= **wasn't**) You/They **were not** hungry. (= **weren't**)

2 명령문: 상대방에게 어떤 행동을 하도록 요구하는 문장으로, 동사원형으로 시작한다.
부정형은 〈Don't + 동사원형〉을 쓴다.

Tell me more about yourself.
Don't tell a lie.

3 청유문: 듣는 사람에게 함께 행동할 것을 제안하는 문장으로, 〈Let's + 동사원형〉으로 시작한다.
부정형은 〈Let's not + 동사원형〉을 쓴다.

Let's get out of here.
Let's not talk about the weather.

- 〈Why don't ~?〉와 같은 의문문의 형태로도 청유문의 의미를 나타낼 수 있다.
  Why don't we meet for lunch on Saturday?

Pop Quiz

A. 빈칸에 알맞은 말을 넣어 부정문을 완성하시오.

1. I like ice cream. → I _____ like ice cream.

2. Kevin saw his brother yesterday. → Kevin _____ see his brother yesterday.

3. Let's stay here. → Let's _____ stay here.

B. 우리말 의미에 맞도록 주어진 단어를 활용하여 문장을 완성하시오.

1. Brian _____ orange juice in the morning. `drink`
   (브라이언은 아침에 오렌지 주스를 마시지 않는다.)

2. _____ to strangers in the elevator. `talk`
   (엘리베이터에서 낯선 사람에게 말을 걸지 마라.)

3. _____ global warming before it is too late! `stop`
   (너무 늦기 전에 지구 온난화를 막읍시다!)

❹ **의문문**: 상대방에게 질문하여 대답을 요구하는 문장으로, 물음표로 끝난다.
의문문에서는 주어와 동사의 위치가 도치된다.

1> Yes나 No로 대답하는 의문문: Be 동사나 Do/Does/Did로 시작한다.

Are you afraid of spiders? – Yes, I am. / No, I am not.
Does Eric like rap music? – Yes, he does. / No, he doesn't.
Did you have a good day? – Yes, I did. / No, I didn't.
Didn't you go to school yesterday? – Yes, I did. / No, I didn't.

2> Yes나 No로 대답하지 않는 의문문: 의문사로 시작하며, 질문에서 요구하는 내용으로 대답한다.

의문사 (Who/What/When/ Where/Why/How)	am	I	not
	am		
	are/is/was/were	주어	
	aren't/isn't/wasn't/weren't		
	do/does/did	주어	동사원형
	don't/doesn't/didn't		

Who is that boy? – He is my son.
Where were you born? – I was born in Bristol, England.
Why didn't Michelle come to school yesterday? – She was sick in bed with a cold.

3> 선택의문문은 Yes나 No로 대답하지 않는다.

Do you go to school by bus or by subway? – I go to school by bus. / By bus.

4> 부가의문문: 긍정문 뒤에는 부정형이, 부정문 뒤에는 긍정형이 온다. 부가의문문이 긍정형이든 부정형이든
이에 대답할 때에는 대답하는 내용이 긍정이면 Yes로, 부정이면 No로 대답한다.

You can't swim, **can you?** – Yes, I can. / No, I can't.
That girl is your sister, **isn't she?** (is not she로 쓰지 않음) – Yes, she is. / No, she isn't.

❺ **감탄문**: **What**이나 **How**로 시작하며, 문장 끝에 느낌표(!)를 쓴다.

• What + (관사) + 형용사 + 명사 + (주어 + 동사) + !   **What** a beautiful gift it is!
• How + 형용사/부사 + (주어 + 동사) + !   **How** fast he runs!

Pop Quiz

A. 빈칸에 알맞은 말을 넣어 의문문을 완성하시오.

1. Monica is pretty. → _____ Monica pretty?

2. Dad is wearing a dark sweater. → _____ is Dad wearing?

3. Their dog barks loudly. → _____ their dog bark loudly?

B. 다음 문장에 알맞은 부가의문문을 쓰시오.

1. It was a fairly hot day, _____?

2. Sally and Lucy don't like Mozart, _____?

3. Your father is not a tall man, _____?

A. 다음 문장을 부정문으로 바꾸어 쓰시오.

1. Grandma drives carefully. → Grandma _____ carefully.

2. You speak German. → You _____ German.

3. Hurry! → _____!

4. My teacher arrived late. → My teacher _____ late.

5. Do the boys play soccer on Sundays? → _____ soccer on Sundays?

B. 다음 문장을 의문문으로 바꾸어 쓰시오.

1. Most children like computer games. → _____ computer games?

2. John and Amy went shopping at the mall. → _____ at the mall?

3. It was raining all day yesterday. → _____ all day yesterday?

4. She got up at 9 this morning. → When _____ this morning?

5. You didn't show up at the dance. → Why _____ at the dance?

C. 다음 문장에 알맞은 부가의문문을 쓰시오.

1. We made a delicious cake yesterday, _____?

2. You plan to open a bakery here, _____?

3. Your brother has two chocolate bars, _____?

4. I didn't turn off my computer, _____?

5. Those kids were rude, _____?

D. 우리말 의미에 맞도록 주어진 단어를 활용하여 문장을 완성하시오.

1. Eagles _____ very beautiful birds.   be
    (독수리는 매우 아름다운 새다.)

2. Math class _____ at 3 o'clock in the afternoon.   end
    (수학 수업은 오후 3시에 끝나지 않는다.)

3. You _____ pizza, do you?   like
    (너는 피자를 좋아하지 않는구나, 그렇지?)

4. _____ puppies you have!   cute
    (너는 정말 귀여운 강아지들을 키우고 있구나!)

5. What time _____?   the concert / start
    (콘서트는 몇 시에 시작하죠?)

3 문장의 주요 성분

1. **주어(Subject)**: 동작이나 상태의 주체가 되는 말로, 명사나 그에 준하는
   표현(대명사, 명사구, 명사절)만이 주어가 될 수 있다.

   Dolphins can swim very fast.
   The hands of the clock are broken.

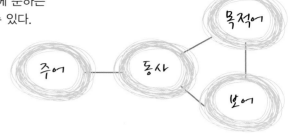

2. **동사(Verb)**: 주어의 동작이나 상태를 나타내는 말을 가리킨다.

   Mike **has** a cat.
   The woman's bag **fell** on the floor.

3. **목적어(Object)**: 동사가 나타내는 동작의 대상을 가리킨다. 명사나 그에 준하는 표현만이 목적어가 될 수 있다.

   Julia loves **you**.
   Please turn off **your cell phone** during the movie.

4. **보어(Complement)**: 주어와 동사만으로 문장의 의미가 완성되지 못할 경우 보충해 주는 말이다.
   주어의 의미를 보충하는 말을 주격보어(SC), 목적어의 의미를 보충하는 말을 목적격보어(OC)라고 한다. 일반적으로 명사와 형용사가 보어가 될 수 있다.

   Adam is **smart and kind**.
   My brother named his dog **Harry Potter**.

✔ 부사구/부사절은 문장의 주요 성분에 해당하지 않는다.
   The train will arrive **in Little Rock at five-thirty**.

Pop Quiz

A. 다음 문장에서 주어를 찾아 밑줄을 그으시오.

1. Sarah cooked spaghetti.
2. Winning the race was not easy for her.
3. What were you doing when I called?
4. Tina is tall and thin.
5. My sister has a pet cat.

B. 다음 문장에서 목적어를 찾아 밑줄을 그으시오.

1. The child was throwing the toys.
2. We bought a lot of food at the supermarket.
3. I enjoy walking in the rain.
4. They read the book during English class.
5. I saw Sandra at the bus stop.

4 동사의 종류와 문장 5형식

4-1 자동사가 있는 문장 (목적어가 필요 없음)

1 **1형식:** 주어(S) + 동사(V)

Birds **fly**.
Carol **ate** alone yesterday.
The post office **closes** early on Saturdays.
Barking dogs never **bite**.
There **is** a kingdom on a cloud. (There는 문장을 이끄는 유도부사이며, is 뒤에 오는 a kingdom이 주어)

2 **2형식:** 주어(S) + 동사(V) + 주격보어(SC)

1> Be 동사

Lillian **is** kind to everyone.
It **was** sunny in the morning.
Worrying about the future **is** a waste of time.
Sally **is** interested in K-pop.
Most frogs **are** green.

2> 감각동사: look, sound, smell, taste, feel, seem 등 (뒤에 형용사 보어가 오는 점에 주의!)

That **sounds** interesting!
Lisa **looks** pretty today.
I **feel** tired and sleepy all day.
The student **seems** angry about something.

3> Become형 동사: become, get, turn, run, grow, come, stay 등

William **became** a dentist.
I **got** upset when I saw Lisa with you.
Jessica **turned** pale at the news.

Pop Quiz

A. 다음 문장에서 동사를 찾아 밑줄을 긋고, 문장이 몇 형식에 해당하는지 쓰시오.

1. The sky turned grey.　　　　　　　　　(　　)
2. Even monkeys fall from trees.　　　　(　　)
3. The cookies were delicious.　　　　　(　　)

B. 괄호 안의 단어 중 알맞은 것을 고르시오.

1. Be (honest / honestly) when you answer the questions.
2. Let's open the window. Something smells (terrible / terribly).
3. Becky never stays (angry / angrily) with me for long.

③ 3형식: 주어(S) + 동사(V) + 목적어(O)

I **love** spring.
The family **spent** the whole day at the zoo.

④ 4형식: 주어(S) + 동사(V) + 간접목적어(IO) + 직접목적어(DO)

Troy **wrote** me a letter.
Amy **told** Steve a secret.

✔ 직접목적어를 먼저 써서 3형식 문장으로 바꾸려면, 간접목적어 앞에 전치사 to, for, of 등을 동사에 어울리도록 써야 한다.
4형식에서 3형식으로 문장 전환시 전치사 to, for, of를 쓸 수 있는 동사 ┌ **to** give, send, show, write, tell
└ **for** buy, make, get, cook
└ **of** ask

My father **bought** me a new cell phone. (4형식)

→ My father **bought** a new cell phone **for** me. (3형식)

⑤ 5형식: 주어(S) + 동사(V) + 목적어(O) + 목적격보어(OC)

1> 목적격보어가 명사인 경우
They call me **Jack**.
The students elected John **president**.

2> 목적격보어가 형용사인 경우
I find this coat really **warm**.
The fog made it **impossible** to find the missing boat.

3> 목적격보어가 부정사인 경우: 지각동사, 사역동사, 기타 불완전타동사
Dora and I **watched** the boys **play** baseball in the park. (원형부정사)
Charley always **makes** us **laugh**. (원형부정사)
Martha **told** her son **to take** out the garbage. (to 부정사)

Pop Quiz

✎ 다음 문장에서 동사를 찾아 밑줄을 긋고, 문장이 몇 형식에 해당하는지 쓰시오.

1. The boy made his little sister cry. (   )
2. Scientists want to discover new planets. (   )
3. Tom gave me a present on my birthday. (   )
4. I asked my mom to feed my dog. (   )
5. Elephants and dogs grow big ears. (   )

A. 다음 문장의 주어를 찾아 밑줄을 그으시오.

1. My mom gives me a hug every morning.
2. Once upon a time, a prince asked a princess, "Will you marry me?"
3. Is English spoken in Canada?
4. There are a dog and three cats inside the house now.
5. Your dreams will come true someday.

B. 다음 문장의 동사를 찾아 밑줄을 긋고, 문장이 몇 형식에 해당하는지 쓰시오.

1. I felt great after taking a nap.   (   )
2. We baked mom a cake.   (   )
3. Leaves turn red and yellow in autumn.   (   )
4. Kevin joined the basketball team.   (   )
5. Accidents will happen.   (   )

C. 주어진 단어들을 알맞게 배열하여 문장을 완성하시오.

1. (with / hair / runs / long / fast)
   → The girl _____.
2. (late / for / yesterday / school / was)
   → Jimmy _____.
3. (Little Prince / the / teaches / lessons / great)
   → A fox _____.
4. (the / paper / floor / the / on / up)
   → Pick _____.
5. (drive / crazy / me)
   → Don't _____.

D. 우리말 의미에 맞도록 주어진 단어를 활용하여 문장을 완성하시오.

1. Steve and Ann _____.   play
   (스티브와 앤은 테니스를 하고 있다.)

2. My brother _____.   find
   (형은 그녀가 매력적이라고 생각한다.)

3. This book _____.   teach
   (이 책은 아이들에게 중요한 교훈을 가르친다.)

4. Andy _____.   write
   (앤디는 여자친구를 위해 노래를 작곡했다.)

5. Patrick _____.   send
   (패트릭이 어제 나한테 장문의 이메일을 보냈다.)

내신 대비 실전문제

이름:		시간: 40분	점수:	/100

선택형 (문항당 3점)

1. 다음 중 문장이 <u>아닌</u> 것은?
① Will you be quiet, please?
② When I was young
③ What an idea!
④ You m-m-must m-m-meet M-M-Mary.
⑤ David said, "Bonjour."

2. 빈칸에 들어갈 말로 알맞은 것은?

> Charlie doesn't _____ chocolate.

① like ② likes
③ liking ④ liked
⑤ to like

3. 빈칸에 들어갈 말로 알맞지 <u>않은</u> 것은?

> Did Matthew _____ yesterday?

① do his homework
② set the table for dinner
③ went to a concert
④ watch TV all day
⑤ have a good time at Peter's party

4. 다음 중 어법상 <u>어색한</u> 것은?
① What a surprise!
② What beautiful flowers they are!
③ What nice weather!
④ How lovely are your eyes!
⑤ How fast she runs!

5. 다음 대화의 질문에 대한 대답으로 알맞은 것은?

> A: Are you interested in American TV shows?
> B: _____

① Yes, you are. ② No, I don't.
③ Yes, I am not. ④ No, I am not.
⑤ No, you aren't.

6. 다음 대화의 질문에 대한 대답으로 알맞지 <u>않은</u> 것은?

> A: Where did you go last weekend?
> B: _____

① Lisa's birthday party.
② I went to Jeju Island.
③ Yes, I had fun at the party.
④ I stayed at home.
⑤ I went to my cousin's wedding.

7. 빈칸에 들어갈 부가의문문으로 알맞은 것은?

> You take a shower every morning, _____?

① don't you ② is it
③ do you ④ aren't you
⑤ isn't it

8. 다음 문장을 부정문으로 옳게 바꾼 것은?

> Tracy fell asleep in math class.

① Tracy isn't fell asleep in math class.
② Tracy doesn't fall asleep in math class.
③ Tracy don't fall asleep in math class.
④ Tracy didn't fall asleep in math class.
⑤ Tracy didn't fell asleep in math class.

9. 다음 의문문으로 바꾼 것 중에서 어법상 <u>어색한</u> 것은?

① Tom was late for school this morning.

→ Was Tom late for school this morning?

② The girls wake up early on Sundays.

→ Does the girls wake up early on Sundays?

③ Jack and Amy made cakes at Lisa's place.

→ Did Jack and Amy make cakes at Lisa's place?

④ The weather is nice today.

→ Is the weather nice today?

⑤ Rob and Sandy always do their homework together.

→ Do Rob and Sandy always do their homework together?

10. 다음 중 어법상 <u>어색한</u> 것은?

① Please careful when you drive.

② Go and get some sleep.

③ Wash your hands before you eat.

④ Don't be late for school again.

⑤ Let me tell you something.

11. 다음 말풍선 ❷에 들어갈 말로 알맞은 것은?

❶ Those are birds, aren't they?

❷ _____

❸ What are they?

❹ They are balloons.

① Yes, they are.

② No, they aren't.

③ Yes, they aren't.

④ No, they are.

⑤ Yes, it is.

12. 다음 중 어법상 <u>어색한</u> 것은?

① There is a lot of water in the bottle.

② There is flowers in the garden.

③ There are many rooms in my house.

④ There is an old computer on the desk.

⑤ There are a lot of birds in the tree.

13. 빈칸에 들어갈 말로 알맞은 것은?

> Mark heard someone _____ his name in the crowded bus.

① call

② called

③ to call

④ calls

⑤ have called

14. 다음 대화의 빈칸에 들어갈 말로 알맞은 것은?

> A: Britney seems _____ these days, doesn't she?
>
> B: Yes, she does. She is taking care of her little brother.

① early

② happily

③ bad

④ exciting

⑤ tired

15. 다음 빈칸에 들어갈 말로 알맞게 짝지은 것은?

> • I saw my grandfather _____ his car.
>
> • I'll have my son _____ care of his little sister.

① fix – take

② fixed – to take

③ fixed – take

④ fix – took

⑤ fixing – to take

16. 다음 중 어법상 어색한 것은?

① How do I look?

② Do they run in the park every day?

③ We usually eat fish on Fridays.

④ Does it taste good?

⑤ The milk smells badly.

17. 다음 중 밑줄 친 부분의 쓰임이 어색한 것은?

① I will help you <u>carry</u> the bag.

② Andrew asked me <u>to pass</u> the ball.

③ Sarah's doctor made her <u>rest</u> in bed for a week.

④ The rain caused many people <u>to run</u>.

⑤ The teacher told his students <u>sing</u> along.

18. 빈칸에 들어갈 말로 알맞지 <u>않은</u> 것은?

> The cafeteria _____ busy at lunchtime.

① is

② happens

③ gets

④ seems

⑤ becomes

19. 다음 중 어법상 옳은 것은?

① The soccer game start at 6:30.

② Kim leave school at 5 every day.

③ That dress looks wonderful.

④ Marcus enjoy fishing on the weekend.

⑤ Finding good friends are hard in a new school.

20. 다음 빈칸에 들어갈 말로 알맞게 짝지은 것은?

> • Einstein's teachers thought him _____.
> • Most Americans consider Lincoln _____.
> • Science made it _____ to get fruits all year round.

① lazy – a hero – possible

② lazy – heroic – possibly

③ lazily – a hero – possibly

④ lazily – heroic – possibly

⑤ lazily – a hero – possible

서술형

21. 다음 빈칸에 공통으로 들어갈 단어를 쓰시오. (3점)

> • Some students _____ learn biology.
> • Sam and Quinn _____ want to go to the Halloween party together.
> • You _____ like bowling, do you?

→ _____

22. 빈칸에 들어갈 알맞은 부가의문문을 쓰시오. (3점)

> The movie was great, _____?

→ _____

23. 다음 중 어법상 어색한 것을 골라 바르게 고쳐 쓰시오. (4점)

> ① I like the puppy in the shop window.
> ② Our math teacher always makes us laughed.
> ③ Charley named his pet Skinny.
> ④ Bring me a glass of water, please.
> ⑤ We painted the house green.

→ _____

24. 사진과 일치하도록 주어진 단어를 알맞게 배열하여
   문장을 완성하시오. (4점)

| or | ride | basketball | bike | play | a |

A: Brian, do you _____

_____ after school

on Mondays?
B: I ride a bike.

25. 다음 문장을 부정문으로 바꾸어 쓰시오. (4점)

> The boy's cough sounded terrible.

→ _____

26. 우리말 의미에 맞도록 문장을 완성하시오. (4점)

> 너는 정말 예쁜 인형을 가지고 있구나!

→ What _____!

27. 주어진 단어를 알맞게 배열하여 문장을 완성하시오. (4점)

| start | fight | not | a |

→ Let's _____!

28. 다음 문장에서 어법상 <u>어색한</u> 부분을 찾아 바르게
   고쳐 쓰시오. (4점)

> Don't let him to pay for dinner.

→ _____

고난도 서술형

29. 우리말 의미에 맞도록 주어진 단어를 활용하여 문장을
   완성하시오. 필요하면 동사의 형태를 바꾸시오. (5점)

> 부모님은 내가 록 콘서트에 가는 것을 허락하지 않았다.

→ My parents _____

to the rock concert. (not / allow / go)

30. 3, 4형식 문장을 찾아 밑줄을 긋고, 이를 주어진
   조건에 알맞게 바꾸어 쓰시오. (5점)

> Hi Aunt Ellen,
> How are you? You sent a wonderful gift to me.
> Thank you very much! My birthday was great.
> Mom and Dad bought me dinner at my
> favorite restaurant. And there was cake for
> dessert. It was delicious.
> Thanks again—see you soon!
> Love,
> Anne

(1) 3형식 → 4형식

   _____

→ _____

(2) 4형식 → 3형식

   _____

→ _____

   _____

Be 동사와 일반동사

Chapter 2

Be 동사와 일반동사

1 Be 동사의 현재형

Be 동사는 인칭과 시제에 따라 형태가 달라지는 가장 대표적인 불규칙 동사로, 존재("~에 있다")나 상태("~이다")를 나타낸다.

주어	긍정	부정	의문
I	am	am not (축약하지 않음)	Am I . . . ?
You	are	are not (= aren't)	Are you . . . ?
He/She/It/단수명사	is	is not (= isn't)	Is he/she/it . . . ?
We/You/They/복수명사	are	are not (= aren't)	Are we/you/they . . . ?

I **am** happy.
Am I late?
You **are** very kind to me.
Are you from Canada?
Lisa **is** from Canada.
The moon **is** in the sky.
Is the coffee hot?
James **isn't** here.
The stores **aren't** open.
Miguel Cabrera and Justin Verlander **are** famous baseball players.

Pop Quiz

 빈칸에 알맞은 be 동사의 현재형을 쓰시오.

1. You _____ a great singer.
2. We _____ 15 years old.
3. _____ Sandy interested in cooking?
4. Fruits and vegetables _____ not expensive.
5. _____ you and Kyle on the soccer team?
6. The TV _____ not too loud.
7. Blue _____ my favorite color.
8. I _____ hungry and thirsty.
9. My sister _____ not taller than me.
10. _____ I your best friend?

2 일반동사의 현재형

1 일반동사의 현재형: 긍정형, 부정형, 의문형

주어	긍정	부정	의문
I/You/We/They/복수명사	do	do not (= don't) + 동사원형	Do I/you/we/they + 동사원형 …?
He/She/It/단수명사	does	does not (= doesn't) + 동사원형	Does he/she/it + 동사원형 …?

My friend Jimmy **speaks** German and English.
Does he **speak** Korean, too?
No, Jimmy **doesn't speak** Korean.
Do Jimmy's parents **speak** Korean?
They **speak** Korean very well.

2 일반동사의 3인칭 단수 현재형 만들기

대부분의 일반동사	원형 + -s
-s, -ch, -sh, -x, -z, -o로 끝나는 동사	원형 + -es
<자음 + -y>로 끝나는 동사	y를 i로 바꾸고 + -es
불규칙 동사	have → has

Tom **plays** the violin.
Liana **has** brown hair.
My dad **does** the dishes in my house.
My mom **teaches** yoga to kids.
Time **flies** like the wind.

Pop Quiz

✏ 괄호 안의 단어 중 알맞은 것을 고르시오.

1. Spaghetti (is / does) not a Japanese food.

2. (Does / Do) Chris have a dog?

3. Kim (carrys / carries) a red backpack.

4. Do spiders (have / has) six legs?

5. The plants (doesn't / don't) need water.

6. Jan (fix / fixes) cars in his free time.

7. Do you (know / knows) my brother?

8. Music (is / do) my new passion.

9. Joe (wash / washes) his hair once a week.

10. Who (does / has) the cooking in your family?

A. 빈칸에 알맞은 단어를 골라 문장을 완성하시오.

have	are	looks	has	does

1. Do your parents _____ blond hair?

2. Maria _____ very angry.

3. _____ it snow in March?

4. _____ the holidays over?

5. Our classroom _____ ten computers.

B. 주어진 단어를 활용하여 현재 시제 문장을 완성하시오.

1. This beach _____ beautiful. be

2. _____ you _____ spicy food? like

3. Teresa's mom _____ to bed early. not go

4. I _____ ready to leave. not be

5. My dad _____ home from work every day. hurry

6. _____ Mel's birthday on April 16? be

7. _____ the teachers _____ Korean? understand

8. Climbing that mountain _____ dangerous. seem

9. The bookstores in my town _____ English books. not have

10. Ken's shirt _____ his shorts. match

C. 우리말 의미에 맞도록 주어진 단어를 활용하여 문장을 완성하시오.

1. Jack and Jill _____ very happy. look
   (잭과 질은 아주 행복해 보이지 않는다.)

2. I _____ chocolate milk. love
   (나는 초콜릿 우유를 좋아한다.)

3. _____ you _____ history interesting? find
   (너는 역사가 재미있니?)

4. This shampoo _____ too much. cost
   (이 샴푸는 너무 비싸다.)

5. Carrie _____ her room very often. clean
   (캐리는 방을 그리 자주 청소하지 않는다.)

③ Be 동사의 과거형

주어가 I/He/She/It/단수명사	was
주어가 We/You/They/복수명사	were

I **was** sick in bed yesterday.
Leonardo da Vinci **was** a famous artist from Italy.
Romeo and Juliet **were** not in school last night.

④ 규칙 동사의 과거형

대부분의 동사	동사원형 + -ed (동사가 -e로 끝나면 + -d)
〈모음 + 자음〉으로 끝나고, 모음이 제1강세를 받으면	자음을 겹쳐 쓰고 + -ed
<자음 + -y>로 끝나면	y를 i로 바꾸고 + -ed

I **played** basketball last weekend.
Tara **lived** in Dayton when she was young.
Mary **stopped** talking when Michael entered the room.
Rachel **tried** her best to save the whale.

Pop Quiz

✎ 다음 동사의 과거형을 쓰시오.

1. like → _____
2. carry → _____
3. drop → _____
4. happen → _____
5. help → _____
6. enjoy → _____
7. solve → _____
8. decide → _____
9. use → _____
10. seem → _____
11. kick → _____
12. wait → _____
13. change → _____
14. show → _____
15. die → _____
16. visit → _____
17. tie → _____
18. reach → _____
19. stay → _____
20. watch → _____
21. live → _____
22. study → _____
23. shop → _____
24. look → _____
25. knit → _____
26. taste → _____

5 불규칙 동사의 과거형과 과거분사형

영어에서 가장 빈번하게 쓰이는 10개의 동사(be, have, do, say, make, go, take, come, see, get)는 모두 불규칙 동사다.

❶ ABB 형

원형	과거형	과거분사형
buy	bought	bought
feel	felt	felt
find	found	found

❷ ABA 형

원형	과거형	과거분사형
come	came	come
run	ran	run

❸ AAA 형

원형	과거형	과거분사형
cost	cost	cost
hit	hit	hit
put	put	put

❹ ABC 형

원형	과거형	과거분사형
begin	began	begun
speak	spoke	spoken
swim	swam	swum

Pop Quiz

✎ 다음 동사의 과거형 및 과거분사형을 쓰시오.

1. forget → _____ → _____
2. hear → _____ → _____
3. write → _____ → _____
4. know → _____ → _____
5. drive → _____ → _____
6. become → _____ → _____
7. let → _____ → _____
8. catch → _____ → _____
9. leave → _____ → _____
10. think → _____ → _____
11. send → _____ → _____
12. bring → _____ → _____
13. take → _____ → _____
14. fly → _____ → _____

Grammar Practice

A. 괄호 안의 단어 중 알맞은 것을 고르시오.

1. I (tried / tryed) to call you last night.
2. The weather (were / was) warmer yesterday.
3. Jack (swam / swum) around the pool three times.
4. Our bus (leaved / left) the station at 9 this morning.
5. The cars (stoped / stopped) at the red light.

B. 주어진 단어를 활용하여 과거 시제 문장을 완성하시오.

1. Mark and I _____ in the computer club last year. be
2. Dana _____ Vicky's gift under her bed. hide
3. The businessman _____ to Tokyo for a meeting. fly
4. As a child, my dad _____ to school every day. walk
5. Uh-oh—I _____ to lock the front door! forget

C. 다음 문장에서 어법상 어색한 부분을 찾아 밑줄을 긋고, 바르게 고쳐 쓰시오.

1. We goed to a big party on Saturday. → _____
2. Math and history was Jenna's favorite subjects. → _____
3. Winter begins early last year. → _____
4. Our new TV costed a lot of money. → _____
5. The teacher spoken to Matthew about his low grade yesterday. → _____

D. 우리말 의미에 맞도록 주어진 단어를 활용하여 문장을 완성하시오.

1. All the seats in the theater _____ taken. be
   (극장 내의 모든 자리는 주인이 있었다.)

2. Kim _____ a wallet full of money on the street. find
   (킴은 길거리에서 돈이 가득 들어 있는 지갑을 발견했다.)

3. We _____ all the floors and windows in the house. wash
   (우리는 집안의 모든 창문과 바닥을 닦았다.)

4. The dog _____ because it wanted to go outside. cry
   (개는 밖에 나가고 싶어서 울었다.)

5. My brother studied hard and _____ a doctor. become
   (우리 오빠는 열심히 공부해서 의사가 되었다.)

선택형 (문항당 3점)

1. 빈칸에 들어갈 말로 알맞은 것은?

> The library _____ closed now.

① was   ② is

③ am   ④ are

⑤ were

2. 다음 빈칸에 들어갈 말로 알맞게 짝지은 것은?

> • Movie stars _____ a lot of money.
> • I _____ understand your question.
> • _____ this shirt look good?

① makes – don't – Does

② make – doesn't – Does

③ make – doesn't – Do

④ makes – don't – Do

⑤ make – don't – Does

3. 다음 중 밑줄 친 부분의 쓰임이 어색한 것은?

① I <u>am</u> in the seventh grade.

② <u>Are</u> your parents at home?

③ Pizza and spaghetti <u>isn't</u> Korean foods.

④ <u>Is</u> milk good for your health?

⑤ The trees <u>aren't</u> very tall yet.

4. 다음 중 어법상 옳은 것은?

① Is a good student he?

② Ned not is polite.

③ Are in your bag the tickets?

④ Am I in your history class?

⑤ The subway crowded isn't today.

5. 다음 중 3인칭 단수의 형태가 <u>잘못된</u> 것은?

① bury – burys

② bake – bakes

③ send – sends

④ have – has

⑤ know – knows

6. 다음 중 어법상 <u>어색한</u> 것은?

① Mom is need a rest this afternoon.

② Eric's cat sleeps on the sofa.

③ Nurses help doctors in hospitals.

④ I have so much homework today.

⑤ Rice and beans taste great together.

7. 다음 의문문으로 바꾼 것 중 어법상 <u>어색한</u> 것은?

① I watch sports on TV.

    → Do I watch sports on TV?

② Brad gets home at 6 p.m. every day.

    → Do Brad get home at 6 p.m. every day?

③ The days become longer in spring.

    → Do the days become longer in spring?

④ You like the color purple.

    → Do you like the color purple?

⑤ Firefighters wear uniforms.

    → Do firefighters wear uniforms?

8. 빈칸에 들어갈 말로 알맞지 <u>않은</u> 것은?

> _____ are great at basketball.

① Sam and I   ② They

③ She and Kyle   ④ You

⑤ He

9. 다음 문장을 부정문으로 옳게 바꾼 것은?

> My sister goes to school by train.

① My sister doesn't goes to school by train.
② My sister don't goes to school by train.
③ My sister doesn't go to school by train.
④ My sister isn't go to school by train.
⑤ My sister isn't goes to school by train.

10. 다음 중 동사의 현재형과 과거형이 <u>잘못</u> 짝지어진 것은?

① mean – meaned
② help – helped
③ fry – fried
④ climb – climbed
⑤ watch – watched

11. 다음 빈칸에 들어갈 말로 알맞게 짝지은 것은?

> • My hair _____ blond five years ago.
> • Billy and Joe _____ in a fight last weekend.

① is – are
② was – were
③ is – was
④ were – was
⑤ are – were

12. 다음 의문문으로 바꾼 것 중 어법상 옳은 것은?

① You were very cute as a baby.
  → Were you very cute as a baby?
② That movie was a big success.
  → Were that movie a big success?
③ It was really cold this morning.
  → Was really cold this morning?
④ Steve wasn't ready for the exam.
  → Was ready Steve for the exam?
⑤ We were late for science class.
  → Were late for science class we?

13. 다음 빈칸에 들어갈 말로 알맞게 짝지은 것은?

> • Pete _____ captain of the team.
> • _____ you angry with me?
> • My new shoes _____ very expensive.

① was – Was – weren't
② were – Was – weren't
③ was – Were – weren't
④ was – Were – wasn't
⑤ were – Were – wasn't

14. 다음 중 동사의 현재형과 과거형이 <u>잘못</u> 짝지어진 것은?

① taste – tasted
② try – tried
③ rush – rushed
④ tap – taped
⑤ work – worked

15. 빈칸에 들어갈 말로 알맞지 <u>않은</u> 것은?

> _____ was popular with students last year.

① Her class
② Red backpacks
③ This restaurant
④ Mr. Hughes
⑤ Hip-hop music

16. 다음 중 어법상 <u>어색한</u> 것은?

① Everyone enjoy your singing last night.
② I thanked the salesman for his help.
③ Kevin plays tennis every Friday.
④ Cats enjoy chasing mice.
⑤ The school day ended early.

17. 다음 빈칸에 들어갈 말로 알맞게 짝지은 것은?

> • _____ you tired this morning?
> • The teacher _____ a research project last Monday.

① Were – assigns
② Are – assign
③ Were – assigned
④ Are – assigns
⑤ Was – assigned

18. 다음 중 동사의 현재형과 과거형이 잘못 짝지어진 것은?

① ring – rang
② put – put
③ catch – caught
④ sing – sung
⑤ write – wrote

19. 빈칸에 들어갈 말로 알맞지 않은 것은?

> Greg _____ Bella's birthday present.

① made   ② brought
③ gotten   ④ bought
⑤ saw

20. 다음 중 동사의 현재형과 과거형이 잘못 짝지어진 것은?

① bring – brought
② find – found
③ show – shown
④ sit – sat
⑤ make – made

서술형

21. 다음 빈칸에 공통으로 들어갈 단어를 쓰시오. (3점)

> • Snow _____ usually fall in May.
> • My essay _____ have any mistakes.
> • Our team _____ practice on Sundays.

→ _____

22. 다음 중 어법상 어색한 문장을 골라 바르게 고쳐 쓰시오. (3점)

> ① The baseball broke the window.
> ② I learned to read at a young age.
> ③ The apartment looked very new.
> ④ We met Muriel at the party.
> ⑤ Nick runned into the house.

→ _____

23. 다음 문장을 부정문으로 바꾸어 쓰시오. (4점)

> I am from a small town.

→ _____

24. 주어진 단어를 알맞게 배열하여 의문문을 완성하시오. (4점)

> Shelly   busy   was

→ _____ last weekend?

25. 다음 문장에서 어법상 어색한 부분을 찾아 바르게 고쳐 쓰시오. (4점)

> Are your chair comfortable?

→ _____

26. 다음 문장을 [보기]와 같이 바꾸어 쓰시오. (4점)

> [보기] I study French.
> → My brother <u>studies</u> German.

I have a small bedroom.

→ Nora _____ a big bedroom.

27. 다음 문장을 부정문으로 바꾸어 쓰시오. (4점)

> The cafeteria food was tasty.

→ _____

28. 다음 문장을 [보기]와 같이 바꾸어 쓰시오. (4점)

> [보기] Our class does a fun project.
> → Our class <u>did</u> a fun project.

The plane leaves on time.

→ _____

29. 우리말 의미에 맞도록 주어진 단어를 활용하여 문장을 완성하시오. (5점)

> 멜라니는 그 어떤 외국어도 할 줄 모른다.

→ Melanie _____

_____. (not speak)

30. 다음 대화를 읽고 밑줄 친 우리말을 영어로 옮겨 쓰시오. (5점)

> A: How was your weekend, Kelly?
> B: It was OK. (1) <u>나는 토요일에 그냥 집에서 텔레비전만 봤어</u>. On Sunday, I went to the park. (2) <u>넌 무엇을 했니</u>, Rob?
> A: I helped my parents at their business. They own a flower shop.

(1) _____

_____

(2) _____

_____

Quattro
Grammar
Start

시제

3 시제

1 현재 시제

1 현재의 상태
Natalie **is** a smart girl.
Matt **has** dark hair.
My sister **thinks** that eating meat is evil.
Jean **doesn't like** animals.

2 현재의 습관
We **play** basketball every weekend.
Kim always **goes** to sleep late on Fridays.
My father and I **walk** in the mountains every Sunday.
I **don't buy** clothes very often.

3 일반적인 사실이나 진리
The sun **rises** in the east.
Ostriches **have** wings, but they **do not fly**.
Boston **is** in the United States.
It **doesn't rain** much in the desert.

4 속담 및 격언
Haste **makes** waste.
A friend in need **is** a friend indeed.
Every dog **has** his day.

Pop Quiz

 주어진 동사를 알맞은 형태로 바꾸어 쓰시오.

1. Bad news _____ fast. travel
2. Zack's eyes _____ blue. be
3. Mrs. Scott _____ French on Mondays. not teach
4. We _____ our friends every summer. visit
5. Kids _____ very fast. grow
6. Peter _____ his car every morning. wash
7. The capital of Thailand _____ Bangkok. be
8. Olivia _____ some famous people. know
9. A bicycle _____ two wheels. have
10. The apple _____ far from the tree. not fall

2 과거 시제

① 과거의 행동이나 상태

It **was** sunny yesterday.
Adam **went** ice skating last weekend.
Claire **lived** in Paris when she **was** young.
Claire **didn't live** in Paris when she **was** young.
Did Adam **go** ice skating last weekend?

② 과거의 습관이나 관습

Stacy **went** to the library every day during her first year in middle school.

✔ used to와 would: 과거의 습관을 나타내는 조동사로, used to는 현재와의 비교에("지금은 그렇지 않다"는 의미를 내포),
would는 반복적인 행위에 초점을 둔다("~하곤 했다"는 의미).

My sister **used to collect** coins, but now she doesn't.
When I was a kid, my father and I **would go** skating every winter.

③ 과거의 역사적 사건 (종종 과거 시점을 나타내는 표현을 수반)

Albert Einstein **was** born on March 14, 1879.
Apollo 11 **flew** to the moon in 1969.
William Shakespeare **wrote** *Romeo and Juliet*.
Did William Shakespeare **write** *Farewell to Arms*, too?
William Shakespeare **didn't write** *Farewell to Arms*.

Pop Quiz

✎ 주어진 동사를 알맞은 형태로 바꾸어 쓰시오.

1. Alice _____ a new pair of shoes yesterday. (buy)

2. We _____ some trees at the park last week. (plant)

3. My friend _____ the cello for nine years. (play)

4. _____ World War II _____ in 1939? (begin)

5. The Beatles _____ a lot of popular songs in the 1960s. (sing)

6. The two girls _____ best friends in elementary school. (not be)

7. Anthony _____ his wallet this morning. (lose)

8. As a kid, I _____ with my sister a lot. (fight)

9. A tsunami _____ Japan in 2010. (hit)

10. Chicago _____ the world's tallest building, but not anymore. (have)

11. _____ you _____ that funny show on TV last night? (see)

12. My mother _____ me a big breakfast this morning. (make)

13. Sam and Mia _____ a gift to their father. (give)

14. I _____ my homework to school. (not bring)

미래 시제와 미래 시제 대용 표현

3-1 will과 be going to

will은 앞으로 일어날 일을 예측하거나 미래의 행위에 대한 의지를 표현할 때 쓴다. **be going to**는 will에 비해 좀 더 가깝고 계획된 일이라는 느낌을 준다.

I **will** be in San Francisco tomorrow morning.
It is cold. I **will** put on a sweater.
If you **are going to** visit London, please bring an umbrella with you.
Look at the clouds in the sky. I think it **is going to** rain soon.
In the year 2050, people **won't** drive cars. (won't = will not)

3-2 미래 시제 대용 표현

❶ 왕래발착 동사(**go, come, leave, arrive, start, end, . . .**)의 경우, 현재 시제나 현재진행 시제가 시간을 나타내는 표현과 함께 쓰여 미래를 표현할 수 있다.

The train **leaves** at 8 in the morning.
Do your parents **arrive** next Monday?
The movie **starts** at 7:30 and 9:30 tonight.
My grandma **is coming** to visit tomorrow.
When **are** you **leaving** for Prague?

❷ 시간 및 조건의 부사절에서는 현재 시제가 미래 시제를 대신한다. 주절에는 미래 시제를 그대로 쓴다.

He will join us when he **finishes** his homework.
When Tom **gets** his driver's license, he will drive his dad's car.
The moment I **arrive** home, I will call you.
If it **rains**, the game will be canceled.

Pop Quiz

A. 괄호 안의 표현 중 알맞은 것을 고르시오.

1. We are going to (graduate / graduating) soon.

2. David is (leave / leaving) for Canada next month.

3. The girls (won't be / will be not) in school tomorrow.

4. If you (will see / see) Hanna, say *hi* to her.

5. Summer (starts / starting) in a couple of weeks.

B. 주어진 동사를 알맞은 형태로 바꾸어 쓰시오.

1. The phone is ringing. I _____ it. (get)

2. In 100 years, the world _____ warmer. (be)

3. I'll go to Christine's party if she _____ me. (invite)

4. The baby's eyes are closing. She _____ asleep. (fall)

5. The new shopping mall _____ on July 20. (open)

Grammar Practice

A. 괄호 안의 표현 중 알맞은 것을 고르시오.

1. Diane often (answers / will answer) questions in class.
2. Fishing (is / has) often a very dangerous job.
3. Over a billion people (live / living) in China.
4. University usually (lasts / last) four years.
5. An apple a day (keeps / kept) the doctor away.

B. 주어진 단어를 알맞게 배열하여 문장을 완성하시오.

1. Everyone _____.
   (the / last / enjoyed / movie / Friday)
2. _____ when I was 7 years old.
   (my / broke / I / arm)
3. Amelia Earhart _____.
   (in / 1930s / pilot / a / famous / was / the)
4. Nora _____, but now it's red.
   (have / used / blond / to / hair)
5. The last Ice Age _____.
   (ago / 10,000 / ended / years)

C. 다음 밑줄 친 부분을 바르게 고쳐 쓰시오.

1. Those bags look heavy; I <u>helps</u> you carry them.   → _____
2. The exam <u>began</u> at 9 a.m. tomorrow.   → _____
3. Let's talk when the meeting <u>will be</u> over.   → _____
4. Around 2100, someone <u>invented</u> a flying car.   → _____
5. My phone battery is at 5 percent now. It <u>died</u> soon.   → _____

D. 우리말 의미에 맞도록 문장을 완성하시오.

1. Robert _____.
   (로버트는 6개월 전에 그 치과의사를 보았다.)
2. If it rains, we _____ for dinner.
   (비가 오면 우리는 저녁식사를 하러 나가지 않을 것이다.)
3. The plane _____ at 4:30.
   (그 비행기는 4시 30분에 서울에 도착한다.)
4. Ivy _____ every day.
   (아이비는 매일 차를 몰고 직장에 간다.)
5. The British _____ in 1814.
   (영국이 1814년에 백악관을 불태웠다.)

4 현재분사와 현재진행

❶ 현재분사 만들기

대부분의 동사	동사원형 + -ing	play → playing sleep → sleeping	send → sending turn → turning
<자음 + -e>로 끝나는 동사	e를 빼고 + -ing	make → making come → coming believe → believing	give → giving take → taking
-ie로 끝나는 동사	ie를 y로 바꾸고 + -ing	lie → lying tie → tying	die → dying
<단모음 + 단자음>으로 끝나는 동사	자음을 겹쳐 쓰고 + -ing	get → getting swim → swimming	stop → stopping run → running

❷ 현재진행: be 동사의 현재형(am/are/is) + 현재분사(-ing)

1> 현재진행 시제는 현재 시점에 벌어지고 있는 동작을 표현할 때 사용한다.

Shirley **is swimming** in the pool.
My father **is washing** the dishes.
What **are** you **doing** here?

2> 현재진행 시제가 미래 시점을 나타내는 표현과 함께 미래의 동작을 나타낼 수 있다.

Zelda **is coming** to the party tonight.
Jason and his students **are leaving** for Egypt next month.

Pop Quiz

A. 다음 동사의 현재분사를 쓰시오.

1. call → _____
2. teach → _____
3. visit → _____
4. build → _____
5. win → _____
6. stand → _____
7. work → _____
8. live → _____
9. fly → _____
10. sit → _____
11. talk → _____
12. choose → _____
13. begin → _____
14. arrive → _____
15. see → _____

B. 괄호 안의 표현 중 알맞은 것을 고르시오.

1. Neil (is take / is taking) taekwondo lessons.
2. Grandma and Grandpa (is sleeping / are sleeping).
3. Light snow (is falling / falls) right now.
4. We are (celebrateing / celebrating) Mom's birthday on Thursday.
5. I am (cutting / cuting) vegetables for dinner.

5 과거진행

과거진행: be 동사의 과거형(was/were) + 현재분사(-ing)

❶ 과거진행 시제는 과거의 특정 시점에 벌어지고 있던 동작을 표현할 때 사용한다.

Joan **was crying** when I saw her today.
We were excited! We **were singing** in the car.
What **were** you **doing** this time yesterday?

❷ 과거진행 시제는 과거의 특정 기간 진행되던 동작을 표현할 때 사용한다.

It **was raining** early this morning.
We **were living** in Florida last year.

6 진행형으로 쓰지 않는 동사들

have, own, belong to, believe, know, like, love, hate, need, seem, feel, taste, sound 등과 같이 소유, 감정, 인식 등 상태를 나타내는 동사들은 진행형으로 쓸 수 없다.

I **am loving** spring. (X) → I **love** spring.
That **is sounding** interesting. (X) → That **sounds** interesting!
Many people **are liking** Disney movies. (X) → Many people **like** Disney movies.

✔ 이 동사들이 동작을 표현할 경우에는 진행형으로 쓸 수도 있다.
Tim **is having** lunch with his brother. (먹고 있다)
The animal doctor **is feeling** the dog's fur. (만져보고 있다)

Pop Quiz

A. 주어진 동사를 알맞은 형태로 바꾸어 쓰시오.

1. The leaves _____ at this time last year. fall

2. We _____ the test when the bell rang. finish

3. I _____ a shower when you knocked on the door. take

4. In March 2012, Kate _____ with her aunt and uncle. stay

5. The sun _____ earlier today. shine

B. 괄호 안의 표현 중 알맞은 것을 고르시오.

1. The dog's nose (feels / is feeling) cold.

2. The two presidents (have / are having) a chat right now.

3. Luckily, Sadie (likes / is liking) her new school.

4. Martin (is looking / looks) like his father.

5. We (enjoy / are enjoying) this nice weather a lot!

7 현재완료

1 현재완료: have/has + 과거분사

긍정형	부정형	의문형
I **have seen** her. He **has seen** her.	I **have not seen** her. (= **haven't seen**) He **has not seen** her. (= **hasn't seen**)	**Have/Haven't** I **seen** her? **Has/Hasn't** he **seen** her?

2 현재완료의 용법

1> 과거에 시작하여 현재까지 계속되는 동작이나 상태를 나타낸다. 일정한 기간을 나타내기 위해 〈for + 시간을 나타내는 명사구〉 또는 과거의 특정 시점을 명시하기 위해 〈since + 명사 또는 절〉을 함께 쓸 수 있다.

Darcy **has lived** in Seoul for seven years.
I **have known** Peggy since kindergarten.
My mother **has not felt** well for the past few months.

2> 과거의 특정 시점 이후 현재까지의 경험을 나타낸다. 경험을 강조하기 위해 ever, never, often 등의 부사를 함께 쓸 수 있다.

I **have never been** to New Zealand.
Have you ever **tried** sushi? – Yes, I have. / No, I haven't.
This is the first time I **have seen** a tiger.

3> 과거에 시작하여 최근에 완료한 일이나 과거에 벌어진 일의 결과를 나타낸다. 의미를 강조하기 위해 just, already, yet, still 등의 부사를 함께 쓸 수 있다.

We **have** just **finished** our project.
I **have lost** my cell phone.
Alex **has forgotten** how to make pancakes.

Pop Quiz

주어진 동사를 알맞은 형태로 바꾸어 쓰시오.

1. That actor _____ in more than twenty movies. be

2. The English language _____ since Shakespeare's time. change

3. _____ Ellen _____ a part-time job? ever / have

4. The young boy _____ in an airplane. never / fly

5. I _____ such a beautiful song in my life. never / hear

6. Several accidents _____ on the icy roads today. happen

7. Michelle _____ in the sun for three hours already. lie

8. My father _____ breakfast for my family. never / make

9. The economy _____ in recent weeks. improve

10. We _____ friends for almost ten years. be

11. _____ Linda _____ you a secret? ever / tell

12. I _____ just _____ home from school. arrive

A. 다음 밑줄 친 부분을 바르게 고쳐 쓰시오.

1. The family is <u>hiked</u> in the mountains tomorrow. → _____
2. The neighbors are <u>played</u> very loud music. → _____
3. I'm <u>made</u> a schedule for next week. → _____
4. Two cats are <u>fight</u> outside right now. → _____
5. Andrew is <u>went</u> to Australia in December. → _____

B. 괄호 안의 표현 중 알맞은 것을 고르시오.

1. Were you (watch / watching) when I scored the goal?
2. Mitch was (waiting / waited) for the bus when the storm started.
3. Lana (closes / closed) the window because she was getting cold.
4. This house (was belonging / belonged) to my grandparents in 2005.
5. April's voice (sounded / was sounding) terrible during the concert.

C. 주어진 동사를 알맞은 형태로 바꾸어 쓰시오.

1. The couple has already _____ a wedding date. pick
2. We're _____ a musical tonight. see
3. Peter's family _____ a large farm. own
4. Joe wasn't _____ any birthday presents. expect
5. Have I ever _____ to you? lie

D. 우리말 의미에 맞도록 주어진 단어를 활용하여 문장을 완성하시오.

1. I _____ my favorite book ten times. read
   (나는 내가 가장 좋아하는 책을 열 번이나 읽은 적이 있다.)

2. Adam _____ us some wonderful news! tell
   (애덤이 방금 우리에게 몇 가지 놀라운 소식을 전해 줬어!)

3. We _____ a topic for our presentation yet. choose
   (우리는 아직 발표 주제를 고르지 못했다.)

4. Your brother _____ how to cook. learn
   (네 오빠는 요리하는 법을 배워 본 적이 없단다.)

5. _____ any Spanish people? meet
   (스페인 사람들을 만나본 적이 있니?)

내신 대비 실전문제

이름: | 시간: 40분 | 점수: /100

선택형 (문항당 3점)

1. 빈칸에 들어갈 말로 알맞은 것은?

   Jane _____ the news every evening.

   ① watch
   ② watching
   ③ is watches
   ④ watches
   ⑤ are watch

2. 다음 중 어법상 <u>어색한</u> 것은?
   ① The coffee shop offers good prices.
   ② Dave and Kelly leads the group.
   ③ A dog is man's best friend.
   ④ Mrs. Granger lives downstairs.
   ⑤ Elephants have curly tails.

3. 다음 중 어법상 옳은 것은?
   ① Sandra waking up early every day.
   ② The Han River run through Seoul.
   ③ Mexico don't have cold weather.
   ④ Gary like to shop at the mall.
   ⑤ We practice our music on weekends.

4. 다음 밑줄 친 동사의 형태로 알맞은 것은?

   Five years ago, Nina <u>sell</u> her car.

   ① sold
   ② sells
   ③ is selling
   ④ will sell
   ⑤ is sell

5. 다음 빈칸에 공통으로 들어갈 말로 알맞은 것은?

   • Lynn and Jeff _____ the laundry.
   • I _____ my homework quickly yesterday.
   • Everyone _____ well on the test last week.

   ① do
   ② does
   ③ did
   ④ are doing
   ⑤ doing

6. 다음 중 밑줄 친 부분의 쓰임이 <u>어색한</u> 것은?
   ① Marianne <u>has hurt</u> her arm a week ago.
   ② The sky <u>looks</u> beautiful tonight.
   ③ I <u>will see</u> you next weekend.
   ④ The fruit <u>fell</u> from the tree.
   ⑤ A bird <u>is building</u> a nest in that tree.

7. 다음 중 어법상 <u>어색한</u> 것은?
   ① I am going to feed the birds.
   ② Ken and Eve are going to growing tomatoes.
   ③ The weather is going to change tomorrow.
   ④ The school festival is going to be on May 15.
   ⑤ The men are going to fix the truck.

8. 다음 문장을 부정문으로 옳게 바꾼 것은?

   Winning the race will be easy for Jerry.

   ① Winning the race will be not easy for Jerry.
   ② Winning the race will not easy be for Jerry.
   ③ Not winning the race will be easy for Jerry.
   ④ Not winning the race easy will be for Jerry.
   ⑤ Winning the race will not be easy for Jerry.

9. 다음 밑줄 친 동사의 형태로 알맞은 것은?

> We'll go when the rain <u>stop</u>.

① stops   ② will stop

③ is stopping   ④ stopped

⑤ is going to stop

10. 다음 중 동사의 현재형과 현재분사형이 잘못 짝지어진 것은?

① feel – feeling

② know – knowing

③ hit – hiting

④ cook – cooking

⑤ try – trying

11. 다음 빈칸에 공통으로 들어갈 말로 알맞은 것은?

> • The library _____ at 8:00 tonight.
> • Pam always _____ the door when she leaves.

① closing   ② close

③ is close   ④ closes

⑤ closed

12. 다음 대화의 질문에 대한 대답으로 알맞은 것은?

> A: Are you working on Sunday afternoon?
> B: _____

① Yes, I do.   ② Yes, I have.

③ Yes, I was.   ④ Yes, I will.

⑤ Yes, I am.

13. 다음 중 밑줄 친 부분의 쓰임이 <u>다른</u> 하나는?

① Sam <u>is going to</u> be tall.

② Sam <u>is going to</u> sing a song.

③ Sam <u>is going to</u> sleep late.

④ Sam <u>is going to</u> the hospital.

⑤ Sam <u>is going to</u> study science.

14. 다음 대화의 질문에 대한 대답으로 알맞은 것은?

> A: I called you ten minutes ago!
> B: Sorry, I didn't hear my phone.
> A: Why not?
> B: _____

① I was listening to music.

② I am listening to music.

③ I listened to music.

④ I have listened to music.

⑤ I listen to music.

15. 다음 의문문으로 바꾼 것 중 어법상 옳은 문장은?

① The sun was shining.

→ Was shining the sun?

② We were having fun.

→ Was we having fun?

③ George and Andy were helping you.

→ Were George and Andy helping you?

④ The pie was baking in the oven.

→ Was the pie was baking in the oven?

⑤ Grandma was reading a story to us.

→ Were Grandma reading a story to us?

16. 다음 중 밑줄 친 부분의 쓰임이 <u>어색한</u> 것은?

① Larry <u>was looking</u> for Greg.

② We <u>were planning</u> a vacation.

③ I <u>was expecting</u> a text from you.

④ The wind <u>was blowing</u> earlier today.

⑤ Rob <u>was hearing</u> that joke already.

17. 다음 중 동사의 현재형과 현재분사형이 잘못 짝지어진 것은?

① tell – telling

② save – saveing

③ catch – catching

④ find – finding

⑤ write – writing

18. 빈칸에 들어갈 말로 알맞은 것은?

> You started practicing yoga in 2010. You still practice yoga.
> → You _____ yoga for three years.

① have practiced   ② practiced

③ practice   ④ are practiced

⑤ will practice

19. 다음 중 동사의 변화형이 잘못 짝지어진 것은?

① come – came – come

② have – had – had

③ hide – hid – hidden

④ catch – caught – caughten

⑤ find – found – found

20. 빈칸에 들어갈 말로 알맞지 <u>않은</u> 것은?

> I've already _____ the flowers.

① chosen   ② seen

③ bought   ④ cut

⑤ grew

21. 두 문장이 같은 뜻이 되도록 빈칸에 알맞은 말을 쓰시오. (3점)

> The teacher seems upset today.

→ The teacher _____ yesterday.

22. 다음 중 어법상 <u>어색한</u> 문장을 골라 바르게 고쳐 쓰시오. (3점)

> ① Tony feels happy today.
> ② The supermarket is selling fresh fruit.
> ③ The cat is chasing a mouse.
> ④ My parents are having a new car.
> ⑤ The students are eating lunch now.

→ _____

23. 다음 빈칸에 들어갈 동사 write의 알맞은 형태를 순서대로 쓰시오. 필요한 경우에는 단어를 추가하시오. (4점)

> • Dan (1) _____ a book last year.
> • Dan (2) _____ a new book now.
> • Dan (3) _____ three books already.

(1) _____

(2) _____

(3) _____

24. 주어진 단어를 알맞게 배열하여 문장을 완성하시오. 필요하면 동사의 형태를 바꾸시오. (4점)

> clean   always   Darla   her room

→ _____ on Sunday evenings.

25. 주어진 단어를 알맞게 배열하여 문장을 완성하시오. (4점)

> never   game   a   has   lost

→ Our soccer team _____

_____ .

26. 다음 그림을 보고, 질문에 알맞은 대답을 완성하시오. (4점)

A: Have you ever tried bungee jumping?

B: No, _____.

27. 우리말 의미에 맞도록 주어진 단어를 알맞게 배열하여 문장을 완성하시오. (4점)

이 마을은 예전에는 작았지만, 현재는 커졌다.

→ _____ small,
but now it is big.
(be / used / the / to / town)

28. 다음 문장을 [보기]와 같이 바꾸어 쓰시오. (4점)

[보기] Marlee played a computer game.
→ Marlee <u>was playing</u> a computer game.

Uncle Edward told a funny story.

→ _____

29. 다음 대화가 완성될 수 있도록 주어진 동사의 알맞은 형태를 순서대로 쓰시오. (5점)

A: I usually (1) _____
(get) good grades in math. But I
(2) _____ (get) a D last
week.

B: Why? What (3) _____
(happen)?

A: I (4) _____ (forget) to
study!

(1) _____

(2) _____

(3) _____

(4) _____

30. 다음 그림과 설명을 보고 세 번째 그림을 상상하여 빈칸을 과거 시제 문장으로 완성하시오. (5점)

Jane was watching a baseball game with her
friend. A player hit the ball, and it came toward
Jane. Then _____

_____

_____.

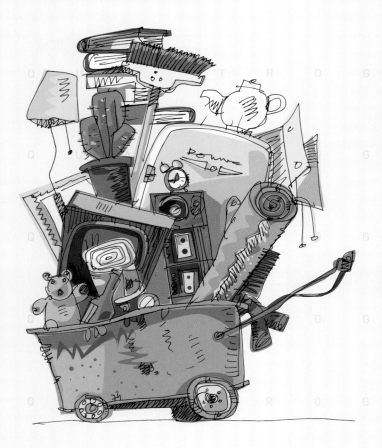

명사와 관사

1. 명사의 종류
2. 명사의 복수형
3. 부정관사와 정관사

명사와 관사

1 명사의 종류

1 셀 수 있는 명사

보통명사: 사람, 동물, 사물	부정관사(a/an)와 함께 쓸 수 있으며, 복수형을 만들 수 있다.	ant, brother, cat, giant, flower, pencil, train, . . .
집합명사: 사람, 동물, 사물의 무리		audience, class, family, team, staff, police, . . .

A giraffe has **a** long **neck**.
The **audience** was excited by the show.
Snakes have no **legs**.

2 셀 수 없는 명사

물질명사: 재료, 물질, 상태	부정관사(a/an)와 함께 쓸 수 없고, 복수형태가 존재하지 않는다.	air, bread, gold, money, paper, water, wood, . . .
추상명사: 추상적인 개념		advice, beauty, friendship, hope, love, peace, . . .
고유명사: 인명, 지명		✔ 대문자로 시작한다. Tom, London, Korea, King's Cross, Steve Jobs, . . .

✔ 물질명사를 세는 단위: 담는 용기나 단위 등을 이용하여 센다 (**a loaf of** bread, **a bottle of** water, **a glass of** milk,
　　　　　　　　　　　　　a piece of chocolate, **a bowl of** soup, **a jar of** peanut butter).

Snow is cold.
Could I have **a glass of water**, please?
Freedom is not free.
Philadelphia is the city of love.

Pop Quiz

 괄호 안의 표현 중 알맞은 것을 고르시오.

1.　This soup needs (a salt / salt).

2.　The baseball broke (a window / window).

3.　(A dentist / Dentist) fixes people's teeth.

4.　I need (a piece / piece) of paper.

5.　Luckily, we have no (homeworks / homework) tonight.

6.　My grandfather always gives me (a good advice / good advice).

7.　Willy bought three (bottle / bottles) of water.

2 명사의 복수형

① 규칙 복수형

대부분의 명사	명사 + -s	alligators, birds, cups, heads, onions, tails, windows, . . .
-s, -x, -ch, -sh, 또는 <자음 + -o>로 끝나는 경우	명사 + -es	buses, foxes, peaches, dishes, potatoes, tomatoes, . . . (예외: pianos, photos)
<자음 + -y>로 끝나는 경우	y를 i로 바꾸고 + -es	babies, candies, parties, stories, . . .
<모음 + -y>로 끝나는 경우	명사 + -s	boys, toys, monkeys, ways, . . .
-f, -fe로 끝나는 경우	f/fe를 v로 바꾸고 + -es	leaves, knives, wives, lives, thieves, wolves, . . . (예외: beliefs, roofs)

② 불규칙 복수형

단수와 복수의 형태가 같은 경우	fish → fish salmon → salmon	sheep → sheep series → series	deer → deer means → means
기타 불규칙 복수형	child → children mouse → mice tooth → teeth	goose → geese oasis → oases woman → women	man → men ox → oxen medium → media

Pop Quiz

다음 명사의 복수형을 쓰시오.

1. lady → _____
2. box → _____
3. elephant → _____
4. fish → _____
5. zoo → _____
6. window → _____
7. thief → _____
8. basis → _____
9. species → _____
10. shrimp → _____
11. church → _____
12. woman → _____
13. mistake → _____
14. month → _____
15. loaf → _____
16. city → _____
17. computer → _____
18. toy → _____
19. mosquito → _____
20. cap → _____
21. truck → _____
22. foot → _____
23. lamb → _____
24. porch → _____
25. day → _____
26. fantasy → _____
27. cloth → _____
28. boss → _____
29. school → _____
30. toe → _____

3 부정관사와 정관사

1 부정관사 a와 an

1> 셀 수 있는 단수 명사 앞에 쓴다.
첫소리가 자음인 단어 앞에서는 a를, 첫소리가 모음인 단어 앞에서는 an을 쓴다. (철자가 아니라 발음 기준)

a boy, **a** man, **a** plan, **a** story, **a** university, **a** zebra, **a** beautiful day, . . .
an ant, **an** egg, **an** island, **an** umbrella, **an** amazing book, **an** MP3 player, . . .

2> 부정관사의 용법: 특정하지 않은 어떤 것을 가리킨다.

하나의(one)	My uncle has **a** son and three daughters.
어떤	Let's find **a** coffee shop.
종족 전체	**A** bicycle has two wheels.
~당(per)	Leslie brushes his teeth three times **a** day.

2 정관사 the: 특정한 대상을 나타내며, 단수 명사와 복수 명사 앞에 모두 쓸 수 있다.

이미 언급한 명사	I saw a spider in my kitchen, so I picked up a fork and threw it at **the** spider.
문맥상 서로 잘 아는 대상	Close **the** window, please.
악기	Can you play **the** guitar?
수식을 받는 명사	Did you see **the** robot that plays the violin?
최상급, 서수, 유일한 사물	Linda is **the** smartest girl in my class.

3 식사, 질병, 운동 앞에는 관사를 쓰지 않는다.

I had **lunch** with Shirley at T.G.I. Friday's.
Steve Jobs died of **cancer** at age 56.
Jenny and Allen play **tennis** every Saturday.

Pop Quiz

✎ 빈칸에 알맞은 관사를 넣어 문장을 완성하시오. 관사가 필요 없으면 ∅ 표시 하시오.

1. There's _____ pharmacy across the street.

2. The storm lasted for over _____ hour.

3. It isn't healthy to skip _____ breakfast.

4. Seoul is _____ biggest city in Korea.

5. There is a bird in the tree. _____ bird is building a nest.

A. [보기]의 물질명사를 세는 단위를 이용하여 테이블 위에 무엇이 놓여 있는지 세어 보시오.

[보기]	glass	bowl	jar	cup	piece

1. _____ of cereal
2. _____ of coffee
3. _____ of milk
4. _____ of bread
5. _____ of juice

B. 괄호 안의 표현 중 알맞은 것을 고르시오.

1. Nathan works for (a university / an university).
2. I've always wanted to learn to play (a violin / the violin).
3. Michelle is going to play (golf / a golf) this weekend.
4. Most men get their hair cut once (a month / the month).
5. My family usually eats (dinner / the dinner) in (kitchen / the kitchen).

C. 주어진 단어들을 알맞게 배열하여 문장을 완성하시오.

1. Please _____.
   (water / a bottle of / me / give)
2. Would _____?
   (a slice of / you / pie / like)
3. Peter _____.
   (rice / two bowls of / ate)
4. We _____.
   (a jar of / used / spaghetti sauce)
5. Mom _____.
   (forgot / bread / a loaf of / to buy)

D. 우리말 의미에 맞도록 주어진 단어를 활용하여 문장을 완성하시오.

1. _____ begins with a smile. peace
   (평화는 미소에서 시작된다.)
2. _____ is bright tonight. moon
   (오늘 밤은 달이 밝다.)
3. Do you have _____? extra pencil
   (연필 남는 것 하나 있니?)
4. Melissa doesn't go to many _____. party
   (멜리사는 파티에 많이 가지 않는다.)
5. There are three TV _____ that I watch every week. series
   (내가 매주 보는 텔레비전 시리즈가 세 개 있다.)

선택형 (문항당 3점)

1. 빈칸에 들어갈 말로 알맞은 것은?

> Some people like _____ too much.

① pet   ② game

③ money   ④ cookie

⑤ snack

2. 빈칸에 들어갈 말로 알맞지 <u>않은</u> 것은?

> There's a piece of _____ on the table.

① soda   ② fruit

③ bread   ④ paper

⑤ chocolate

3. 다음 중 어법상 <u>어색한</u> 것은?

① We enjoy our free time.

② Soda is bad for your health.

③ Tom doesn't wear glasses.

④ Alexandra has five uncle.

⑤ A man is knocking on the door.

4. 다음 중 셀 수 <u>없는</u> 명사를 모두 고르시오.

① knowledge   ② building

③ computer   ④ snow

⑤ idea

5. 빈칸에 들어갈 말로 알맞지 <u>않은</u> 것은?

> Everyone wants to have _____.

① parties   ② friends

③ fun   ④ happiness

⑤ holiday

6. 다음 빈칸에 들어갈 말로 알맞게 짝지은 것은?

> • Two _____ of bread are in the bag.
> • Add a _____ of sugar to the pan.
> • This _____ of cake is too big!

① pieces – glass – jar

② bottles – spoonful – slice

③ pieces – spoonful – slice

④ bottles – slice – jar

⑤ loaves – slice – jar

7. 다음 중 명사의 단수형과 복수형이 잘못 짝지어진 것은?

① room – rooms

② man – mans

③ tie – ties

④ cello – cellos

⑤ plate – plates

8. 다음 중 셀 수 <u>없는</u> 명사를 모두 고르시오.

① child   ② potato

③ air   ④ money

⑤ year

9. 다음 중 명사의 단수형과 복수형이 잘못 짝지어진 것은?

① party – partys

② play – plays

③ toy – toys

④ day – days

⑤ boy – boys

10. 다음 중 밑줄 친 부분의 쓰임이 옳은 것은?

① <u>Parents</u> take care of children.

② Many tourists visit <u>the</u> Rome.

③ <u>Sky</u> is grey and cloudy today.

④ I'll have <u>the</u> cup of coffee, please.

⑤ Little kids cannot drive <u>the</u> cars.

11. 다음 빈칸에 들어갈 말로 알맞게 짝지은 것은?

- I'd like _____ egg with my toast.
- _____ airplane is landing.
- Let's see _____ movie on Saturday.

① an – An – a

② a – An – a

③ an – An – an

④ a – A – an

⑤ an – A – an

12. 다음 중 어법상 옳은 것은?

① Nelly's favorite color is the blue.

② We enjoy lying in the sun.

③ Tony is taking the shower.

④ Rabbits have the soft fur.

⑤ Don't eat the fast food every day.

13. 다음 중 명사의 단수형과 복수형이 잘못 짝지어진 것은?

① wife – wives

② loaf – loaves

③ knife – knives

④ shelf – shelves

⑤ belief – believes

14. 다음 중 어법상 <u>어색한</u> 것은?

① Please close the window.

② Mom is reading an old book.

③ Deer are beautiful animals.

④ Take a breaks if you're tired.

⑤ Gail wants to play the drums.

15. 빈칸에 들어갈 말로 알맞지 <u>않은</u> 것은?

My brother has a _____.

① idea

② headache

③ puppy

④ girlfriend

⑤ problem

16. 다음 중 밑줄 친 부분의 쓰임이 옳은 것은?

① Your toys are on <u>a</u> floor.

② <u>The</u> kindness is important.

③ Aaron wears <u>a</u> orange scarf.

④ This is <u>an</u> useful book.

⑤ Jill is <u>the</u> girl next to Michael.

17. 다음 중 명사의 단수형과 복수형이 잘못 짝지어진 것은?

① deer – deer

② fish – fish

③ species – species

④ mouse – mouse

⑤ sheep – sheep

18. 빈칸에 들어갈 말로 알맞지 <u>않은</u> 것은?

Cameron is eating a _____ in the park.

① hot dog

② lunch

③ sandwich

④ meal

⑤ salad

19. 다음 중 어법상 옳은 것은?

① A world has seven billion people.

② I visit my dentist twice a year.

③ Teresa lives near a elementary school.

④ We saw a elephant at the zoo.

⑤ Yesterday we had a easy test.

20. 빈칸에 들어갈 말로 알맞지 <u>않은</u> 것은?

Celia knows a lot about the _____.

① moon

② Internet

③ pop music

④ best restaurants in town

⑤ history of Korea

서술형

21. 다음 중 밑줄 친 부분의 쓰임이 <u>어색한</u> 것을 골라 바르게 고쳐 쓰시오. (3점)

① <u>Homework</u> is often boring.

② We were late because of <u>traffics</u>.

③ Their apartment has two <u>bedrooms</u>.

④ <u>Chickens</u> cannot fly.

⑤ France makes good <u>wine</u>.

→ _____

22. 다음 중 밑줄 친 부분의 쓰임이 <u>어색한</u> 것을 골라 바르게 고쳐 쓰시오. (3점)

① <u>James</u> is always smiling.

② Denise is <u>the</u> youngest girl in her family.

③ People wear <u>boot</u> in the rain.

④ I like to watch <u>baseball</u> on TV.

⑤ <u>Trees</u> change color in the fall.

→ _____

23. 다음 대화의 빈칸에 알맞은 관사를 순서대로 쓰시오. (4점)

A: Can you help me write (1) _____ report for school?

B: Sure. What is (2) _____ report about?

A: American holidays.

(1) _____

(2) _____

24. 다음 중 셀 수 있는 명사를 골라 쓰시오. (4점)

cheese	spoon	sentence
doll	honesty	water

→ _____

25. 주어진 단어를 알맞게 배열하여 문장을 완성하시오. (4점)

shared   bowl   a   popcorn   of

→ Marie and I _____

_____ .

26. 다음 문장을 [보기]와 같이 바꾸어 쓰시오. (4점)

[보기] A woman is singing.
→ Three <u>women are</u> singing.

A child is playing on the grass.

→ Three _____

_____ .

27. 다음 문장에서 어법상 <u>어색한</u> 부분을 찾아 바르게 고쳐 쓰시오. (4점)

Mark will visit four citys on his trip.

→ _____

28. 다음 문장에서 어법상 <u>어색한</u> 부분을 찾아 바르게
고쳐 쓰시오. (4점)

> This pair of shoe costs $30.

→ _____

29. 다음 그림과 설명을 보고, 질문에 알맞은 대답을 완성
하시오. (5점)

A: Look at this photo. Which one is your teacher?

B: My teacher is _____.
  (우리 선생님은 파란 셔츠를 입은 남자야.)

30. 다음 글을 읽고 빈칸에 알맞은 관사를 순서대로 쓰시오. (5점)

> ## NEW COMPUTER LAB
>
> Central Public Library has (1) _____
> excellent new computer lab. (2) _____ lab
> is on the second floor. It has thirty computers,
> three printers, and two scanners. Use of all the
> equipment is free. However, you must have
> (3) _____ library card. Please go to
> (4) _____ front desk for more information.

(1) _____

(2) _____

(3) _____

(4) _____

Quattro
Grammar
Start

대명사

① 인칭대명사

① 인칭대명사의 종류

	주격	소유격	목적격	소유대명사	재귀대명사
단수	I	my	me	mine	myself
	you	your	you	yours	yourself
	he	his	him	his	himself
	she	her	her	hers	herself
	it	its	it		itself
복수	we	our	us	ours	ourselves
	you	your	you	yours	yourselves
	they	their	them	theirs	themselves

② 인칭대명사의 용법

1> 인칭대명사는 사람을 지칭하거나 사람의 이름을 대신한다.
Claire, **you** look pretty today.
Adam is very smart, and **he** is a great basketball player. (Adam → he)

2> 인칭대명사의 주격은 문장에서 주어로 쓰이며, 목적격은 동사나 전치사의 목적어로 쓰인다.
I don't want to go to the dentist.
Grandma always tells **us** amazing stories.

3> 인칭대명사의 소유격은 명사를 꾸며주며, 소유대명사는 〈소유격 + 명사〉를 줄인 것이다.
Amy and **her** brother have a pet rabbit.
Their rabbit is bigger than **mine**. (mine = my rabbit)

4> 재귀대명사는 문장의 주어와 목적어가 같을 때 목적어 자리에 쓴다.
명사 뒤나 문장 끝에서 강조 용법으로도 쓰는데, 이때 재귀대명사는 생략할 수 있다.
Karen is looking at **herself** in her mother's mirror.
Enjoy **yourself** at the party. (명령문의 주어 you와 목적어가 일치)
Let's make the birthday cake **ourselves**.

Pop Quiz

🖊 빈칸에 알맞은 단어를 골라 문장을 완성하시오.

him	his	yourself	she	their

1. Peter likes Jenny a lot, and I think _____ likes him, too.

2. I will visit my grandparents, and my friend Joe will visit _____.

3. The Johnsons invited us to _____ apartment for dinner.

4. Mr. Woods asked us to call _____ Ken.

5. Be careful on the ice, or you'll hurt _____.

2 지시대명사

가까이 있는 사람이나 사물	단수	this
	복수	these
멀리 있는 사람이나 사물	단수	that
	복수	those

This is my brother Matthew.
Is **this** your cell phone? – Yes, it is. / No, it isn't.
These are not shoes. They are sandals.
Hurry up! **That** is my school bus.
Those are my friends.

✔ 명사 앞에서 그 명사를 수식하는 지시형용사로 쓰이기도 한다.
Do you like **this** shirt?
These flowers are for my girlfriend.
Look at **those** pictures.

3 비인칭 It

날씨	How's the weather today? – **It** is a beautiful day. **It** will rain tomorrow.
시간	What time is **it**? – **It**'s 5:30. What day is **it**? – **It**'s Wednesday. What's the date today? / What's today's date? – **It**'s May 15.
거리	How far is **it** from here to the nearest subway station? **It**'s about 500 meters.

Pop Quiz

A. 빈칸에 알맞은 단어를 골라 문장을 완성하시오.

this	that	these	those

1. What are _____ things in the sky?

2. Please give me _____ bag under your chair over there.

3. Let me introduce you. _____ are my parents, Mr. and Mrs. Shin.

4. Look at _____ hole in my shirt!

B. 밑줄 친 it의 용법을 쓰시오.

1. <u>It</u>'s a long way from Earth to the moon.   (   )

2. <u>It</u>'s 7 o'clock in the morning.   (   )

3. <u>It</u>'s getting warmer.   (   )

A. 빈칸에 알맞은 인칭대명사를 쓰시오.

    1. Emily and Kelly are sisters, but _____ don't look similar.

    2. I always enjoy _____ at Helen's parties.

    3. Victor remembered his textbook, but Nina forgot _____.

    4. We are all sad that Mindy isn't going to _____ school anymore.

    5. The windows are open. Please close _____ before you leave.

B. 괄호 안의 단어 중 알맞은 것을 고르시오.

    1. (This / These) is Valerie's favorite song.

    2. Why don't you try on (this / these) jeans?

    3. (These / Those) people in that car are waving at us.

    4. Please pick up (that / this) piece of paper over there.

    5. Let's leave. (This / That) movie is really boring.

C. 주어진 단어를 알맞은 형태로 바꾸어 쓰시오.

    1. What's _____ name? she

    2. Lou doesn't like looking at _____ in the mirror. he

    3. Is the long black coat _____? you

    4. What a beautiful dog! I love _____ soft fur. it

    5. Jim ran for president, but they elected _____ vice-president instead. he

D. 의문사 what이나 how를 사용하여 다음 대답에 알맞은 질문을 쓰시오.

    1. A: _____
        B: It's noon.

    2. A: _____
        B: It's three miles.

    3. A: _____
        B: It's April 16th.

    4. A: _____
        B: It's sunny and hot.

    5. A: _____
        B: It's Friday.

 **4 의문대명사**

1 Who

주격 (누가)	소유격 (누구의)	목적격 (누구를)	소유대명사 (누구의 것)
who	whose	whom (who)	whose

1> 사람의 이름, 신분, 관계 등을 묻는다.

Who is that tall boy? – He is my brother, Brian.
Who are you? – I am Batman.
Who are they? – They are my grandparents.

2> Whose: 소유격(형용사) 및 소유대명사로 쓰인다.

Whose dog is this? – It's my sister's.
Whose is this song? – It's Adele's.

3> Whom: 목적격으로 쓰이며, 구어체 영어에서는 종종 who를 쓴다.

Who(m) are you waiting for?

2 **What** [주격 및 목적격]: 동물 및 사물에 관해 물을 때 사용하며, 명사를 수식하는 의문형용사로도 쓰인다.

What is the name of your pet dog?
What can I do for you?
What food do you hate the most?

3 **Which** [주격 및 목적격]: 사람, 동물, 사물의 정해진 대상 중에서 하나를 선택하는 질문에 사용하며, 명사를 수식하는 의문형용사로도 쓰인다.

Which is better for my health, running or walking?
Which do you like better, ice cream or coffee?
Which animal do you want to raise, a turtle or a hamster?

Pop Quiz

빈칸에 알맞은 의문대명사 또는 의문형용사를 쓰시오.

1. _____ was the name of the first person who walked on the moon?
2. _____ artwork is this? I'd like to ask him or her about it.
3. _____ did you choose for a partner?
4. _____ subject do you prefer, history or science?
5. _____ color are Kelly's eyes?
6. _____ gave you that book?
7. _____ bedroom is this? It's so messy.
8. _____ do you usually drink, juice or soda?

5 부정대명사

1 One: 앞에서 언급한 불특정한 사람이나 사물을 지칭한다.

My cell phone is too slow. I need to buy a new **one**.

✔ 특정한 대상을 언급할 때에는 it을 쓴다.
My cell phone is too slow. I need to fix **it**.

2 Some을 포함한 부정대명사: some, somebody, someone, something

I'm hungry. I want **something** to eat.
Somebody came to see you this morning.

✔ some은 명사를 수식하는 부정형용사로도 쓰인다.
Would you like **some** candy?

3 Any를 포함한 부정대명사: anybody, anyone, anything

Is there **anybody** home?
I can't see **anything** without my glasses.

✔ any는 명사를 수식하는 부정형용사로도 쓰인다.
Did you hear **any** news about Edward?

4 Every를 포함한 부정대명사: everybody, everyone, everything

Tara gave chocolates to **everyone** in her class.
My brother already ate **everything** good.

5 No를 포함한 부정대명사: nobody, nothing

Nobody knows that you are a robot, not a man.
There is **nothing** I can do to help you.

Pop Quiz

✎ 빈칸에 알맞은 단어를 골라 문장을 완성하시오.

> something   nobody   anything   anyone   everything   everyone   some   someone   one   nothing

1. Jared hasn't eaten _____ all day.

2. There isn't _____ taller than you in our class.

3. Chris likes our new car, but I liked our old _____ better.

4. I'm thirsty, but there's _____ to drink!

5. It's a beautiful day. We should do _____ fun outside.

6. I have _____ good news about our midterm exam.

7. Did _____ call while I was in the shower?

8. _____ loves chocolate except me.

9. _____ came to Monica's party, so she was depressed.

10. There isn't any more tea left. You already drank _____.

A. 빈칸에 알맞은 부정대명사를 쓰시오.

1. Everyone is shouting, so I can't hear _____.
2. Mom called the doctor's office, but _____ answered.
3. Jerry ate a lot of cake, and I didn't get _____!
4. Be careful on your trip. Don't do _____ dangerous.
5. This cafe is much more expensive than that _____.

B. 빈칸에 알맞은 의문대명사를 쓰시오.

1. _____ kinds of books do you like to read?
2. _____ is your homeroom teacher this year?
3. _____ do you admire the most?
4. _____ hair is the longest in your family?
5. _____ is healthier, Korean food or French food?

C. 괄호 안의 표현 중 알맞은 것을 고르시오.

1. Tell me (something / someone) about your father.
2. (Whom / Whose) phone is ringing?
3. (Who / What) is the best student in our class?
4. (What / Which) is a better time to visit Australia, January or July?
5. I haven't met (anyone / no one) interesting for a long time.

D. 다음 대답에 알맞은 질문을 쓰시오.

1. A: _____

   B: We saw **Mr. Lim** at the festival.

2. A: _____

   B: **No**, I have nothing to do right now.

3. A: _____

   B: That's **Mary-Jane's** desk.

4. A: _____

   B: **No**, nobody is in the bathroom.

5. A: _____

   B: **Purple** is my favorite color.

내신 대비 실전문제

| 이름: | | 시간: 40분 | 점수: | /100 |

선택형 (문항당 3점)

1. 다음 중 밑줄 친 부분을 대명사로 바꾼 것 중 어색한 것은?
   ① <u>Lisa and I</u> are hungry. (→ Us)
   ② <u>Mrs. James</u> lives next door. (→ She)
   ③ <u>My room</u> is a mess. (→ It)
   ④ <u>The two brothers</u> look alike. (→ They)
   ⑤ <u>You and your friend</u> can sit here. (→ You)

2. 다음 중 밑줄 친 부분을 생략할 수 있는 것은?
   ① I see <u>myself</u> in the photo.
   ② The kids taught <u>themselves</u>.
   ③ The body can heal <u>itself</u>.
   ④ Sally made her dress <u>herself</u>.
   ⑤ Mark is so proud of <u>himself</u>.

3. 다음 중 밑줄 친 부분을 대명사로 바꾼 것 중 어색한 것은?
   ① Please wash <u>your hands</u>. (→ them)
   ② Mom punished <u>my brother and me</u>. (→ us)
   ③ Say hello to <u>Alicia</u>. (→ her)
   ④ I quickly spoke to <u>your uncle</u>. (→ his)
   ⑤ We never watch <u>that TV show</u>. (→ it)

4. 다음 중 빈칸에 들어갈 수 없는 것은?

   • The camera is _____.
   • _____ owns the camera.
   • He bought the camera _____.

   ① she   ② her
   ③ his   ④ himself
   ⑤ hers

5. 다음 빈칸에 들어갈 말로 알맞게 짝지은 것은?

   • They enjoyed _____ very much.
   • This table is _____.
   • That's John's picture. _____ painted it.

   ① themselves – we – He
   ② they – ourselves – Him
   ③ they – ours – He
   ④ themselves – us – Him
   ⑤ themselves – ours – He

6. 다음 중 밑줄 친 부분을 대명사로 바꾼 것 중 어색한 것은?
   ① Math is <u>Molly's</u> best subject. (→ her)
   ② <u>The car's</u> tires are flat. (→ Their)
   ③ Most of <u>Hawaii's</u> turtles are green turtles. (→ its)
   ④ <u>Jacob's</u> grades are the best. (→ His)
   ⑤ <u>The book's</u> author became famous. (→ Its)

7. 다음 대화의 빈칸에 들어갈 말로 알맞지 <u>않은</u> 것은?

   A: Whose flowers are these?
   B: They're _____.

   ① his   ② mine
   ③ your   ④ hers
   ⑤ theirs

8. 빈칸에 들어갈 말로 알맞은 것은?

   _____ room is too hot.

   ① This   ② Them
   ③ These   ④ Those
   ⑤ It

9. 다음 중 밑줄 친 부분의 쓰임이 옳은 것은?

① <u>It</u> are my new sunglasses.

② <u>These</u> is good candy.

③ <u>That</u> were difficult questions.

④ <u>Those</u> are my pet goldfish.

⑤ <u>It</u> were interesting speeches.

10. 다음 중 어법상 <u>어색한</u> 것은?

① This homework is easy.

② Those stars are so bright.

③ That men look angry.

④ This salad tastes great.

⑤ These children need help.

11. 다음 빈칸에 들어갈 말로 알맞게 짝지은 것은?

- I don't like _____ ice cream.
- Look at _____ two deer!
- _____ are the baby's toys.

① this – those – These

② these – that – These

③ these – that – This

④ this – those – This

⑤ this – that – These

12. 다음 대화의 질문에 대한 대답으로 알맞지 <u>않은</u> 것은?

A: Whose money is this?
B: _____

① It's mine.

② It's yours.

③ It's his.

④ It's theirs.

⑤ It's him.

13. 다음 중 밑줄 친 it의 쓰임이 <u>다른</u> 하나는?

① <u>It</u> is 100 kilometers to the capital.

② <u>It</u> is a brand-new library.

③ <u>It</u> is Thursday.

④ <u>It</u> is cool and rainy.

⑤ <u>It</u> is 6:45 p.m.

14. 다음 대화의 질문에 대한 대답으로 알맞은 것은?

A: What is this?
B: _____

① They're water bottles.

② We're sleepy.

③ It's a birthday present.

④ She's my cousin.

⑤ You're a little late.

15. 빈칸에 들어갈 말로 알맞은 것은?

_____ is the title of that book?

① What　　　　　② Which

③ Whom　　　　 ④ Whose

⑤ Who

16. 다음 대화의 질문에 대한 대답으로 알맞은 것은?

A: Whom does Andrea like?
B: _____

① My sister likes her.

② I like Andrea.

③ She doesn't like Gary.

④ She likes Bobby.

⑤ Everyone likes her.

17. 다음 중 빈칸 어디에도 들어갈 수 없는 것은?

> • I don't see _____ wrong.
> • Is _____ in the kitchen?
> • Would you like _____ to drink?

① someone   ② anyone

③ anything   ④ nothing

⑤ something

18. 다음 중 밑줄 친 부분의 쓰임이 다른 하나는?

① We're almost out of napkins. <u>One</u> is left.

② Marty has four sisters, and I have <u>one</u>.

③ The used TV is cheaper than the new <u>one</u>.

④ I have a lot of pens, but I only need <u>one</u>.

⑤ Don't take so many candies; just take <u>one</u>.

19. 다음 중 어법상 옳은 것은?

① Everyone are here.

② Anybody made a mess.

③ I'd like everyone to talk to.

④ Everybody needs exercise.

⑤ We hear anyone talking.

20. 다음 빈칸에 들어갈 말로 알맞게 짝지은 것은?

> • Did you learn _____ new today?
> • _____ stole my bag!
> • I asked everyone, but _____ knew the answer.

① something – Anybody – everybody

② anything – Somebody – nobody

③ anyone – Somebody – somebody

④ anything – Anybody – nobody

⑤ something – Somebody – everybody

21. 다음 대화의 빈칸에 들어갈 알맞은 말을 쓰시오. (3점)

> A: _____ is more popular, comedy or drama?
> B: I think comedy is more popular.

→ _____

22. 다음 대화의 밑줄 친 부분과 바꾸어 쓸 수 있는 대명사를 쓰시오. (3점)

> A: Which shirt do you want?
> B: I prefer the striped <u>shirt</u>.

→ _____

23. 다음 중 밑줄 친 부분의 쓰임이 어색한 것을 골라 바르게 고쳐 쓰시오. (4점)

> ① I need time, but I don't have <u>any</u>.
> ② <u>Someone</u> is calling me right now.
> ③ Let's eat <u>something</u> tasty.
> ④ Jamie knows <u>any</u> famous.
> ⑤ Do you have <u>anything</u> to read?

→ _____

24. [보기]와 같이 괄호 안의 단어를 알맞게 바꾸어 빈칸에 쓰시오. (4점)

> [보기] <u>Her</u> uniform is new. (← She)

(1) _____ shoes are wet. (← we)

(2) _____ face is red. (← you)

(3) _____ smile is nice. (← he)

25. 다음 빈칸에 공통으로 들어갈 단어를 쓰시오. (4점)

> • Is _____ warm today?
>
> • What day is _____?
>
> • _____ is 4 o'clock.

→ _____

26. 다음 대화의 빈칸에 들어갈 알맞은 말을 쓰시오. (4점)

> A: _____ teaches piano lessons?
>
> B: Mrs. Kraus.

→ _____

27. 다음 대화의 빈칸에 들어갈 알맞은 말을 쓰시오. (4점)

> A: What do you want to do tomorrow?
>
> B: Let's do _____ relaxing.

→ _____

28. 다음 대화의 밑줄 친 부분을 <u>두 단어</u>로 바꾸어 쓰시오. (4점)

> A: Whose desk is this?
>
> B: It is <u>hers</u>.

→ _____

29. [보기]와 같이 재귀대명사로 문장을 완성하시오. (5점)

> [보기] He talks to <u>himself</u>.

(1) Cats clean _____.

(2) I almost hurt _____.

(3) We like to hear _____ sing.

30. 다음 대화를 읽고 밑줄 친 대명사가 각각 무엇을 의미하는지 쓰시오. (5점)

> A: I found this pencil case on the floor. Is it yours, Mia?
>
> B: No, it's not. (1) <u>Mine</u> is in my bag.
>
> A: Whose is it, then? Do you know?
>
> B: Maybe it's Heejin's. It's pink, and that's (2) <u>her</u> favorite color.
>
> A: OK, I'll ask her.

(1) Mine: _____

(2) her: _____

Quattro
Grammar
Start

형용사와 부사

형용사와 부사

 1 형용사의 기본 용법

형용사는 명사를 꾸며주는 말로 명사의 성질이나 상태를 나타낸다. 그 위치에 따라 명사 앞이나 뒤에서 직접 꾸며주는 한정적 용법과, 동사 뒤에서 주어나 목적어를 보완하는 서술적 용법으로 나뉜다.

> Ms. Windsor is **my favorite** teacher. (한정적 용법)
> Tim watched a **great** movie on TV. (한정적 용법)
>
> Diamond rings are **expensive**. (서술적 용법–주격보어)
> Duncan wanted his coffee **black**. (서술적 용법–목적격보어)

 2 수량 형용사

> **All** the dishes were delicious. (수)
> **Most** women enjoy chatting with friends. (수)
> **Many** colleges seek creative students. (수)
> The recipe needs **a few** ingredients. (수–긍정)
> My mother has **few** health problems. (수–부정)
> I brought **some** interesting books for you. (수)
>
> Greg spent **all** his money on gambling. (양)
> **Most** food is safe for a few days after it's cooked. (양)
>
> Linda speaks **a little** Korean. (양–긍정)
> The boy drinks **little** milk. (양–부정)
> Can you buy **some** milk for me? (양)

> ✔ a lot of(= lots of)는 수와 양에 모두 쓸 수 있으며, 주로 긍정문에 쓰인다. 부정문에서는 many(수)나 much(양)가 주로 쓰인다.
> Ken wants to make **a lot of** money. (양) (a lot of = much)
> **A lot of** people buy hybrid cars. (수) (a lot of = many)
> Bananas don't have **much** fat in them. (양)

Pop Quiz

A. 다음 문장에서 형용사를 찾아 밑줄을 긋고, 어떤 용법으로 쓰였는지 쓰시오.

1. Mozart is a famous composer. ( )
2. The bag looks heavy. ( )
3. The night was cold. ( )
4. The ribbon makes the dress beautiful. ( )

B. 다음 문장에서 수량 형용사를 찾아 밑줄을 긋고, 수와 양 가운데 무엇을 나타내는지 쓰시오.

1. There are some eggs in the refrigerator. ( )
2. Gillian has few friends here. ( )
3. There's a little caffeine in herbal tea. ( )
4. People don't eat much meat in India. ( )
5. Most children enjoy playing with animals. ( )

3 형용사의 비교급과 최상급

① 비교급, 최상급 만들기: 규칙 변화

	비교급 / 최상급	예
단음절	형용사 + -er / -est	high – higher – highest fast – faster – fastest small – smaller – smallest old – older – oldest
〈단모음 + 단자음〉으로 끝날 때	자음을 겹쳐 쓰고 + -er / -est	big – bigger – biggest hot – hotter – hottest fat – fatter – fattest
2음절이며 -y로 끝나는 경우	y를 i로 바꾸고 + -er / -est	pretty – prettier – prettiest easy – easier – easiest happy – happier – happiest naughty – naughtier – naughtiest
기타 2음절 이상	more / most + 원급	important – more important – most important unusual – more unusual – most unusual perfect – more perfect – most perfect expensive – more expensive – most expensive

② 비교급, 최상급 만들기: 불규칙 변화

good/well – better – best
bad/ill – worse – worst
many/much – more – most
far – farther(거리)/further(정도) – farthest/furthest

Pop Quiz

다음 형용사의 비교급과 최상급을 쓰시오.

1. dangerous → _____ → _____
2. quick → _____ → _____
3. common → _____ → _____
4. clean → _____ → _____
5. painful → _____ → _____
6. cheap → _____ → _____
7. useful → _____ → _____
8. beautiful → _____ → _____
9. rapid → _____ → _____
10. comfortable → _____ → _____
11. difficult → _____ → _____
12. thin → _____ → _____
13. shiny → _____ → _____
14. tall → _____ → _____

4 형용사와 비교 구문

1 원급 비교 구문: as + 형용사 + as + 비교 대상

Mark is **as healthy** as Doreen.
Learning English is **as difficult as** swimming.
The dog is **not so/as fast as** the cat. (부정)
English is **not so/as difficult as** Arabic. (부정)

2 비교급을 이용한 비교 구문: 형용사 비교급 + than + 비교 대상

My brother is **lazier than** I am. (구어체에서는 I am 대신 me를 쓰기도 함)
The studio is **smaller than** the one-bedroom apartment.
My cat is **prettier than** yours.
Shopping online is **not more convenient than** shopping in a store. (부정)

✔ 비교급 앞에 much, even, still, far, a lot 등을 써서 "훨씬"이라는 뜻을 나타낼 수 있다.
Junk foods are **much cheaper** than healthy foods.
The Internet made the world **a lot more awesome**.

3 최상급 구문: <of + 비교 대상>이나 <in/on + 장소> 등의 표현이 함께 나올 수 있다.

Diane is **the most respected** teacher **in the school**.
The easiest subject for Molly is mathematics.
The most successful pop group **of all time** was the Beatles.
The cheapest food **on the menu** is a hamburger.

Pop Quiz

✎ 주어진 표현을 활용하여 문장을 완성하시오. 필요하면 단어의 형태를 바꾸거나 다른 단어를 추가하시오.

1. Naples is _____ as Rome. `not / fantastic`

2. Milk is _____ than soda. `healthy`

3. Joe's brother is _____ than he is. `outgoing`

4. Winter is _____ than summer. `not / enjoyable`

5. Brad seems _____ nowadays. `far / happy`

6. My new school is _____ than my old one. `even / big`

7. Who was _____ actress of all time? `famous`

8. My younger sister is _____ as my older brother. `not / fast`

9. Picasso is _____ artist I've heard of. `unique`

10. Tom's jokes are _____ than my jokes. `funny`

11. This is _____ cake I've ever eaten. `delicious`

12. Running on a treadmill is _____ as running outside. `not / challenging`

13. My favorite singer's new song is _____ than her last one. `good`

14. Seoul is _____ city in Korea. `exciting`

A. 문장의 주어와 어울리도록 주어진 동사의 현재 시제를 빈칸에 쓰시오.

1. All the coffee _____ gone. be
2. Most students in Korea _____ uniforms. wear
3. There _____ some coins in my wallet. be
4. A lot of people _____ this movie. hate
5. Little rain _____ in the desert. fall

B. 주어진 단어들을 알맞게 배열하여 문장을 완성하시오.

1. Katelyn _____.
   (excellent / is / artist / an)
2. My dad's job _____.
   (tired / him / makes)
3. William _____.
   (Chinese / finds / difficult)
4. This store _____.
   (nice / a / clothes / of / lot / sells)
5. The soup _____.
   (a / needs / salt / little)

C. 주어진 형용사를 알맞은 형태로 바꾸어 쓰시오.

1. Pumpkins are a lot _____ than tomatoes. large
2. Larissa is _____ person in her family. friendly
3. My room was not _____ as yours. messy
4. Nick tells much _____ stories than I do. interesting
5. Soccer is _____ sport in the world. popular

D. 우리말 의미에 맞도록 주어진 형용사를 활용하여 문장을 완성하시오.

1. Debbie is _____ her older brother. hardworking
   (데비는 오빠만큼 부지런하다.)
2. My grandmother has _____ smile. lovely
   (우리 할머니는 가장 사랑스러운 미소를 지으신다.)
3. Snowboarding seems _____ skiing. exciting
   (스노보드가 스키보다 더 재미있어 보인다.)
4. Carlos isn't _____ he was two years ago. shy
   (카를로스는 2년 전만큼 부끄러워하지 않는다.)
5. I think snakes are _____ animals of all. frightening
   (나는 뱀이 동물 중에서 제일 징그럽다고 생각한다.)

5 부사의 형태

1 부사의 규칙적 형태

대부분의 부사	형용사 + -ly	polite – politely kind – kindly quiet – quietly
-y로 끝나는 형용사	y를 i로 바꾸고 + -ly	heavy – heavily pretty – prettily angry – angrily
-ic로 끝나는 형용사	형용사 + -ally	fantastic – fantastically energetic – energetically
-le로 끝나는 형용사	e를 빼고 + -ly	terrible – terribly responsible – responsibly

✔ -ly로 끝나지만 부사가 아니라 형용사로 주로 쓰이는 경우
Beth is a **lovely** girl.
That dress is **ugly**.
John felt **lonely**.

2 형용사와 부사의 형태가 같은 경우: early, fast, late, hard 등
The **early** stamps cost only a penny. (형용사)
My sister always goes to bed **early**. (부사)
Joel is a **fast** driver. (형용사)
Jean drives **fast**. (부사)

Pop Quiz

A. 다음 형용사의 알맞은 부사 형태를 쓰시오.

1. incorrect → _____
2. enthusiastic → _____
3. sad → _____
4. shy → _____
5. beautiful → _____
6. creative → _____
7. quick → _____
8. lucky → _____
9. careful → _____
10. historic → _____

B. 괄호 안의 단어 중 알맞은 것을 고르시오.

1. Peggy studies (hard / hardly) for the exam.
2. The runners came very (late / lately).
3. The family has an (early / earlily) dinner.
4. Carrie is a (fast / fastly) runner.
5. Lanh came home (early / earlily).

6 부사의 역할

1 동사 수식

Does your father drive **carefully**?
Jeremy walked **quietly** into the church. (= Jeremy **quietly** walked into the church.)

2 형용사 수식

That was a **really** exciting movie.
Don't you think the puppies are **very** cute?

3 다른 부사(구) 수식

We don't talk **very** loudly in class.
The plane flew **high** above the clouds. (부사구 역할을 하는 전치사구 above the clouds를 수식)

4 절 또는 문장 전체 수식

Recently, I have lost my beloved puppy.
The baby fell asleep **immediately** after her favorite TV show was over. (after 이하의 부사절을 수식)

7 빈도부사

빈도부사는 Be 동사나 조동사의 뒤, 일반동사의 앞에 온다.

0%						100%
never	hardly ever	rarely/seldom	sometimes	often	usually	always

Larry is **never** on time.
Bill **rarely** uses public transportation.
Rainstorms may **often** happen before monsoon season.
George **usually** goes shopping at the mall near house.
Warren **always** gets up early in the morning.

Pop Quiz

✎ 주어진 빈도부사를 알맞은 위치에 넣어 문장을 다시 쓰시오.

1. Dinner is served with wine. (usually)

   → _____

2. Jenny can be seen in the cafeteria. (often)

   → _____

3. You could depend on me to help you out. (always)

   → _____

4. Jimmy visits his parents during the school year. (hardly ever)

   → _____

8 부사구와 부사절

1 **부사구**: 두 개 이상의 단어가 모여 문장의 주요 성분이 아닌 부사의 역할을 한다.

   1> 전치사 + 명사

   Jane worked on the project **with care**. (= carefully)
   Jane worked on the project **without care**. (= carelessly)
   I usually read novels **for fun**. (목적)
   Larry came home **around eight**. (시간)
   Jason put the chairs away **in the garage**. (장소)
   Her mother looks young **for her age**. (비교)

   • Hannah found a book **of interest** in the library. (<of + 명사>는 부사가 아닌 형용사 역할)

   2> to + 동사원형

   Faye came home early **to see the game**. (목적)
   Kristen was surprised **not to find her dad** at home. (원인)
   My mother would be happy **to meet you**. (조건)
   My grandma was too slow **to take the bus**. (형용사 수식)

2 **부사절**: 〈종속접속사 + 주어 + 동사〉의 형태로 문장의 의미를 보완하며, 문장의 주요 성분은 아니다.

   I called a taxi **because I needed to get home quickly**. (이유)
   Before we buy a new computer, we should decide how much we want to spend. (시간)
   Although Hernando was born in Spain, he doesn't speak Spanish. (양보)
   If it rains, I can't ride my bike to school. (조건)

Pop Quiz

✎ 부사구 또는 부사절에 해당하는 부분에 밑줄을 긋고, 그 부분을 우리말로 옮겨 쓰시오.

1. I went to the bank to cash a check.   _____

2. Nancy has been a teacher for a long time.   _____

3. Tim left early in order to avoid the traffic jam.   _____

4. Vince lifts weights at the gym.   _____

5. We keep our dishes under the kitchen sink.   _____

6. I studied until I fell asleep.   _____

7. Jack doesn't talk to girls because he is shy.   _____

8. If you save money, you can buy new clothes.   _____

9. Although whales look like fish, they are not.   _____

10. Allen didn't answer the phone because
     he didn't want to talk to his mother.   _____

A. 괄호 안의 단어 중 알맞은 것을 고르시오.

1. We all thought that Jane sang (beautiful / beautifully).
2. Paul's mother bought him a (new / newly) suit.
3. My roommate is sleeping, so we should talk (quiet / quietly).
4. Gene feels (awful / awfully) because he has a bad cold.
5. Who answered the question (correct / correctly)?

B. 우리말 의미에 맞도록 문장을 완성하시오.

1. They usually eat dinner _____.
   (그들은 보통 부엌에서 밥을 먹는다.)
2. Rosie is saving her money _____.
   (로지는 차를 사기 위해 돈을 모으고 있다.)
3. The kids were excited _____ at the zoo.
   (아이들은 동물원에서 사자를 보자 신이 났다.)
4. Two men were arguing _____.
   (두 남자는 매우 시끄럽게 다투고 있었다.)
5. I'm usually in a good mood _____.
   (나는 보통 금요일 오후에는 기분이 좋다.)

C. 다음 문장에서 어법상 어색한 부분을 찾아 밑줄을 긋고, 바르게 고쳐 쓰시오.

1. Ariel plays seldom computer games. → _____
2. Haejin went to bed sometimes before midnight. → _____
3. Hardly ever teenagers marry in this country. → _____
4. Never there is enough food for everyone. → _____
5. I will be always your friend. → _____

D. 우리말 의미에 맞도록 주어진 동사를 활용하여 문장을 완성하시오.

1. The train _____ crowded during rush hour. be
   (기차는 종종 통근시간에 굉장히 붐빈다.)
2. Mrs. Green _____ us difficult quizzes. give
   (그린 선생님은 가끔 우리에게 어려운 퀴즈를 내준다.)
3. It _____ still dark at 5 a.m. be
   (보통 오전 5시에는 여전히 깜깜하다.)
4. Chris is very serious and _____. smile
   (크리스는 매우 신중하고 거의 웃지 않는다.)
5. My favorite baseball team _____ the championship. win
   (내가 제일 좋아하는 농구팀은 우승을 차지한 적이 한 번도 없었다.)

선택형 (문항당 3점)

1. 다음 중 yellow가 들어가기에 알맞은 위치는?

> Kimberly ① lent ② her ③ sweater ④ to ⑤ me.

①   ②   ③   ④   ⑤

2. 다음 중 어법상 어색한 것은?

① Mom's soup is spicy.
② Bill wants his soup spicy.
③ They eat spicy soup.
④ This is spicy soup.
⑤ I made spicy the soup.

3. 빈칸에 들어갈 말로 알맞은 것은?

> A _____ toys are on the floor.

① few   ② lot
③ most   ④ all
⑤ many

4. 빈칸에 들어갈 말로 알맞지 <u>않은</u> 것은?

> My friend Ben did _____ homework.

① some   ② few
③ a little   ④ all his
⑤ a lot of

5. 다음 중 far가 들어가기에 알맞은 위치는?

> ① Dark hair ② is ③ more ④ common ⑤ than red hair.

①   ②   ③   ④   ⑤

6. 다음 중 형용사의 비교급과 최상급이 잘못 짝지어진 것은?

① boring – more boring – most boring
② modern – moderner – modernest
③ pretty – prettier – prettiest
④ white – whiter – whitest
⑤ dangerous – more dangerous – most dangerous

7. 다음 빈칸에 들어갈 말로 알맞게 짝지은 것은?

> • Cancer is a _____ disease.
> • Laura's problem is _____ than mine.

① more serious – the most serious
② serious – the most serious
③ the most serious – more serious
④ serious – more serious
⑤ more serious – serious

8. 빈칸에 들어갈 말로 알맞은 것은?

> Yesterday was _____ day of the year.

① rainy   ② rainier
③ the rainiest   ④ the rainier
⑤ rainiest

9. 다음 중 밑줄 친 부분의 쓰임이 옳은 것은?

① Mark is <u>the thiner</u> person in the group.
② These hats are <u>more ugly</u> than those.
③ Apple pie is <u>the tastier</u> dessert I've ever had.
④ The stars look <u>bright</u> than they did last night.
⑤ Clara was <u>the tallest</u> of the three sisters.

10. 다음 중 형용사의 비교급과 최상급이 잘못 짝지어진 것은?
① small – smaller – smallest
② helpful – more helpful – most helpful
③ wet – wetter – wettest
④ new – newer – newest
⑤ dirty – more dirty – most dirty

11. 빈칸에 들어갈 말로 알맞은 것은?

Is Mr. Noh as _____ as his wife?

① intelligent
② intelligenter
③ more intelligent
④ most intelligent
⑤ the most intelligent

12. 빈칸에 들어갈 말로 알맞지 <u>않은</u> 것은?

London is a big city, but Seoul is _____ bigger.

① even   ② much
③ a lot   ④ very
⑤ still

13. 빈칸에 들어갈 말로 알맞지 <u>않은</u> 것은?

Peter spoke _____ at the meeting.

① nicely   ② lovely
③ strangely   ④ badly
⑤ politely

14. 다음 중 짝지어진 두 단어의 관계가 나머지와 <u>다른</u> 하나는?
① entire – entirely
② late – late
③ public – publicly
④ friend – friendly
⑤ humble – humbly

15. 다음 빈칸에 들어갈 말로 알맞게 짝지은 것은?

• You worked _____ to finish on time.
• Rudeness makes most people _____.
• Noel caught the ball _____.

① hardly – angry – easy
② hard – angry – easily
③ hard – angrily – easily
④ hardly – angry – easily
⑤ hard – angrily – easy

16. 빈칸에 들어갈 말로 알맞지 <u>않은</u> 것은?

Uncle Timothy takes photos _____.

① wonderful
② with his new camera
③ terribly
④ in the morning
⑤ to remember his trips

17. 다음 중 very가 들어가기에 알맞은 위치는?

Mona ① became ② the ③ class ④ president ⑤ recently.

①   ②   ③   ④   ⑤

18. 다음 대화의 질문에 대한 대답으로 알맞지 <u>않은</u> 것은?

A: How often do you read comic books?
B: _____

① Often.
② Quickly.
③ Rarely.
④ Hardly ever.
⑤ Very seldom.

19. 빈칸에 들어갈 말로 알맞은 것은?

Are you afraid _____ on the roller coaster?

① go
② to go
③ to going
④ be going
⑤ have gone

20. 다음 중 어법상 옳은 것은?

① Always Monique's winter clothes are stylish.
② Monique's always winter clothes are stylish.
③ Monique's winter always clothes are stylish.
④ Monique's winter clothes are always stylish.
⑤ Monique's winter clothes are stylish always.

서술형

21. 다음 중 밑줄 친 부분의 쓰임이 어색한 것을 골라 바르게 고쳐 쓰시오. (3점)

① All the flowers <u>have</u> died.
② Most bottled water <u>are</u> cheap.
③ Few animals <u>are</u> smarter than whales.
④ Some rice <u>is</u> still in the bowl.
⑤ There <u>is</u> a little paint on your shirt.

→ _____

22. 다음 빈칸에 들어갈 말을 순서대로 쓰시오. (3점)

- Gary isn't as handsome (1) _____ his older brother.
- Your backpack might be more expensive (2) _____ mine.
- What was (3) _____ most exciting part of the movie?

(1) _____

(2) _____

(3) _____

23. 다음 문장의 알맞은 위치에 **usually**를 넣어 다시 쓰시오. (4점)

I go to the market with my parents.

→ _____

24. 다음 문장에서 어법상 <u>어색한</u> 부분을 찾아 바르게 고쳐 쓰시오. (4점)

Nina is trying to correct all the mistake in her essay.

→ _____
_____

25. 우리말 의미에 맞도록 문장을 완성하시오. (4점)

버스 정류장이 지하철보다 가깝다.

→ The bus stop is _____ the subway station.

26. 다음 밑줄 친 단어를 바르게 고쳐 쓰시오. (4점)

The businessman often travels <u>international</u>.

→ _____

27. 두 문장이 같은 뜻이 되도록 빈칸에 알맞은 단어를 쓰시오. (4점)

The package arrived. It was early.

→ The package arrived _____.

28. 우리말 의미에 맞도록 주어진 단어를 알맞게 배열하시오. (4점)

> 데릭은 과학 수업이 전혀 지루하지 않다.

→ _____

_____

(is / bored / never / in / Derek / science class)

고난도 서술형

29. 다음 글을 읽고 주어진 형용사를 활용하여 요약문을 완성하시오. (5점)

> I have two best friends, Hyunwoo and Jaemin. Hyunwoo is really smart and shy. Jaemin is also smart, but he's not as smart as Hyunwoo. And he's not shy! Jaemin is very friendly and outgoing. On the other hand, Jaemin is not as funny as Hyunwoo. They're both nice guys, but they're very different.

↓

> [**Summary**]
> Hyunwoo is (1)_____ (smart) and (2) _____ (funny) than Jaemin. But Jaemin is (3) _____ (outgoing) than Hyunwoo.

(1) _____

(2) _____

(3) _____

30. 다음 도표는 어느 반의 학생들이 어떤 음료를 좋아하는지를 조사한 것이다. 이 도표와 일치하도록 "popular"를 활용하여 문장을 완성하시오. (5점)

Drink	Number of Students
Soda	13
Tea	9
Juice	11
Water	9

(1) Juice is _____

than tea.

(2) Tea is _____

as water.

(3) Soda is _____

drink of the four.

조동사

조동사

1 조동사의 종류와 기본 용법

조동사는 다른 동사와 결합하여 그 동사의 형태와 의미를 보완하는 역할을 한다.

1 다른 동사의 형태를 보완하는 조동사

1> Be 동사: 현재분사와 결합하여 진행형을, 과거분사와 결합하여 수동태를 만든다.
Chris **is having** a lot of fun right now. (진행형)
This book **was written** by Alain de Botton. (수동태)

2> Do 동사: 부정문과 의문문을 만들 때, 또는 동사를 강조할 때 쓴다.
Joshua **doesn't like** the new bike. (부정문)
Do you **want** your coffee without sugar? (의문문)
Chris dances very well. – You're right. He **does** dance well! (강조)

3> Have 동사: 현재완료, 과거완료, 미래완료 시제에 쓰인다.
We **haven't met** for a long time. (현재완료)
Sue **had been** a nurse before she became a pilot. (과거완료)
Kim **will have finished** cleaning up by the time we get home. (미래완료)

2 법조동사: 다른 동사와 결합하여 능력, 추측, 허가, 의무, 의지 등 주어의 태도를 나타내는 역할을 하는 조동사를 법조동사라 한다. 좁은 의미의 조동사는 바로 법조동사를 가리킨다.

Bad things **can** happen to good people. (가능성)
Hummingbirds **can** fly backwards. (능력)
Orlando **will** be late for tomorrow's meeting. (예측)
You **may** go inside now. (허락)
You **must** have a secret. (강한 추측)
I don't know why this machine **would** not take my money. (고집)
Employers **should** not ask about your race or religion. (금지: not과 함께 쓰일 경우)

Pop Quiz

 다음 문장에서 조동사를 찾아 밑줄을 그으시오.

1. By exercising, you can build strength.

2. Do you want to go for a ride?

3. I will meet you for lunch tomorrow.

4. Anna wasn't sleeping then.

5. Have you finished your lunch yet?

6. The forest may disappear for good.

7. Jodi was shocked at the news.

8. Michael has won five medals for his country.

2 법조동사의 쓰임새

① 법조동사 뒤에는 반드시 동사원형을 쓴다.

Ryan can **learn** other languages very easily.
You had better **hurry**, or you'll miss breakfast.

② 법조동사의 부정형, 축약형, 의문형

법조동사	부정형	축약형	의문형	대답
can	cannot	can't	Can you ~?	Yes, I can. / No, I can't.
will	will not	won't	Will you ~?	Yes, I will. / No, I won't.
may	may not	—	May I ~?	Yes, you may. / No, you may not.
must	must not	mustn't	Must I ~?	Yes, you must. / No, you don't have to
should	should not	shouldn't	Should I ~?	Yes, you should. / No, you shouldn't.
would	would not	wouldn't	Would you ~?	Yes, I would. / No, I wouldn't.
might	might not	—	Might I ~?	Yes, you might. / No, you might not.
had better	had better not	—	Had I better ~?	Yes, you'd better. / No, you'd better not.
have to	do not have to	don't have to	Do I have to ~?	Yes, you do. / Yes, you have to. / No, you don't have to.

You **may not get** a present this Christmas.
You **cannot stay** here any longer. (can not으로 띄어 쓰지 않음)
Will you **lend** me your umbrella?
When can we **see** the rainbow?
They**'ll come** along in a moment.
You **shouldn't do** anything else while studying.
She **won't sign** up for the competition.
Couldn't you **speak** more slowly, please?
You **mustn't disturb** your sister now.

Pop Quiz

✎ 다음 문장을 괄호 안에 제시된 형태로 바꾸어 쓰시오.

1. We can live to be one hundred. (의문문)
    → _____

2. I may use the Internet for a while. (의문문)
    → _____

3. There might be ice cream for dessert. (부정문)
    → _____

4. Would you like to take a walk before dinner? (부정문)
    → _____

5. Sungmin has to take the exam again. (부정문)
    → _____

3 법조동사의 종류 I

● 능력, 가능성: can, could, be able to, will be able to

Regina **can** speak Korean very well. (현재)
Regina's father **could** speak Korean and Chinese. (과거)
Regina **will be able to** speak Chinese as well. (미래)
You **can** easily get lost in the dark. (일반적인 가능성)
You **can** make a lot of money if you are lucky. (현실적인 가능성)
People **could** starve in those days. (과거의 일반적인 가능성)

✔ 과거 특정 시점의 능력을 나타낼 때에는 could보다 was/were able to가 더 자연스럽다.
   Jeff **was able to** get two tickets to the concert.
   Matt stood in line for over an hour, but he **couldn't** get the tickets. (부정문에서는 couldn't도 상관 없음)
   (= Matt stood in line for over an hour, but he **wasn't able to** get the tickets.)

4 법조동사의 종류 II

● 허가, 제안, 금지, 추측, 의무, 조언, 습관: may, will, can, must, shall, might, would, should, had better, have to

May I use your cell phone? (허가)
Shall we begin the meeting? (제안)
You **can't** take food into the museum. (금지)
Maybe it **will** rain this afternoon. (추측 = It might rain this afternoon.)
Maya **has to** complete the test in thirty minutes. (의무)
You **should** be careful when you cross the street. (조언)
Nicole **had better** start eating healthier food. (조언)
Samuel **would** sleep on his father's lap when he was a child. (과거의 습관)

Pop Quiz

✎ 괄호 안의 표현 중 알맞은 것을 고르시오.

1. Look—you (can / could) see the ocean from this window.
2. Not everyone (could / had better) go to school in the past.
3. Kim (is / was) able to speak a little Spanish when she was young.
4. You (might / have to) be able to get a student discount.
5. Sorry, I'm busy today. But I will (can / be able to) help you tomorrow.
6. I could run five kilometers a year ago, but I (can't / couldn't) now.
7. You (had better / has to) not lose your phone again.
8. When I was living in Boston, I (would / might) walk to work.

A. 빈칸에 알맞은 단어를 골라 문장을 완성하시오.

is	does	did	have	can

1. _____ you say goodbye to Alicia last night?
2. This door _____ locked at the end of every day.
3. We live near the airport, so we _____ hear the planes.
4. I was wrong before. South Africa _____ have three capital cities.
5. _____ you heard about Justin Bieber before?

B. 두 문장이 같은 뜻이 되도록 빈칸에 알맞은 조동사를 쓰시오.

1. People have to recycle and save energy.
   → People _____ recycle and save energy.
2. Maybe we will see Sam today.
   → We _____ see Sam today.
3. It is not necessary for Patrick to pay the bill.
   → Patrick _____ pay the bill.
4. Taking photos is not allowed here.
   → People _____ take photos here.
5. Why don't you take a hot bath?
   → You _____ take a hot bath.

C. 괄호 안의 표현 중 알맞은 것을 고르시오.

1. Kim Yuna could (skate / skating) when she was seven.
2. Will is sneezing and coughing. He must (has / have) a cold.
3. According to the news, it (won't / mustn't) snow this weekend.
4. Luckily, we (could / were able to) catch the last train on Friday.
5. Learning (can / had better) be fun if the topic is interesting.

D. 우리말 의미에 맞도록 주어진 동사를 활용하여 문장을 완성하시오.

1. You _____ my things without asking.   borrow
   (내 물건을 허락 없이 빌려가면 안 돼.)
2. As adults, we _____ more decisions for ourselves.   make
   (어른이 되면 우리는 스스로 더 많은 결정을 내릴 수 있을 것이다.)
3. Amanda _____ the boots to the store.   return
   (아만다는 부츠를 가게에 반환해야 한다.)
4. Mom and Dad _____ a babysitter yesterday.   find
   (엄마와 아빠는 어제 아이 봐 줄 사람을 찾을 수 있었다.)
5. Your computer is slow. You _____ removing some programs.   try
   (네 컴퓨터는 느려. 프로그램 몇 개를 제거해 봐야겠어.)

내신 대비 실전문제

이름: 시간: 40분   점수: /100

선택형 (문항당 3점)

1. 다음 중 밑줄 친 단어를 알맞은 형태로 바꾼 것은?

Erica is lived here for ten years.

① are   ② was

③ were   ④ have

⑤ has

2. 다음 대화의 밑줄 친 부분 중 어법상 옳은 것은?

A: ① Will you lending me a pencil?
B: Sorry. I ② aren't have a pencil, but I ③ do have a pen.
A: ④ I'll doing a crossword puzzle, so I ⑤ should use not ink.

①　　　②　　　③　　　④　　　⑤

3. 빈칸에 들어갈 말로 알맞지 <u>않은</u> 것은?

Matthew ＿＿＿＿＿＿＿＿ quit his job soon.

① might   ② is going to

③ may   ④ won't

⑤ have to

4. 다음 중 어법상 <u>어색한</u> 것은?

① Farmers don't usually sleep late.

② These shoes aren't too expensive.

③ We haven't to cook dinner tonight.

④ People shouldn't drink too much soda.

⑤ I won't tell anyone your secret.

5. 다음 빈칸에 들어갈 말로 알맞게 짝지은 것은?

• ＿＿＿＿＿＿＿＿ you exercise yesterday?
• Brook ＿＿＿＿＿＿ never been to Daegu since 1999.

① Did – has

② Have – has

③ Have – did

④ Did – is

⑤ Were – is

6. 빈칸에 들어갈 말로 알맞은 것은?

The TV should not ＿＿＿＿＿＿＿ so loud.

① be   ② is

③ was   ④ are

⑤ were

7. 다음 중 밑줄 친 부분의 쓰임이 <u>다른</u> 하나는?

① I <u>can't</u> remember the meaning of this word.

② You <u>can't</u> leave the table until dinner is over.

③ My uncle <u>can't</u> play any musical instruments.

④ Animals <u>can't</u> live without food and water.

⑤ Jack <u>can't</u> beat Ellen at table tennis.

8. 빈칸에 들어갈 말로 알맞지 <u>않은</u> 것은?

A lot of students are ＿＿＿＿＿＿ at that university.

① taught   ② studying

③ work   ④ living

⑤ educated

9. 다음 중 어법상 <u>어색한</u> 것은?

① Children under 18 must not drive.

② Teresa may not know the answer.

③ The package might not arrive.

④ Dogs does not eat chocolate.

⑤ We had better not fall asleep.

10. 두 문장이 같은 뜻이 되도록 할 때 빈칸에 알맞은 말은?

Maybe Natalia will be president of her country someday.
= Natalia _____ be president of her country someday.

① would
② might
③ has to
④ should
⑤ must

11. 빈칸에 공통으로 들어갈 말로 알맞은 것은?

• The girls _____ get dressed.
• You _____ wear your glasses.
• I _____ rest for a minute.

① used to
② have to
③ was able to
④ do
⑤ has to

12. 다음 대화의 질문에 대한 대답으로 알맞은 것은?

A: Elliott wants to stay and help us clean up. Is that necessary?
B: _____

① No, he couldn't.

② No, he won't.

③ No, he must not.

④ No, he wasn't able to.

⑤ No, he doesn't have to.

13. 다음 대화의 빈칸에 들어갈 말로 알맞은 것은?

A: Let's make plans for this weekend. What do you want to do?
B: Hmm. _____ we see a movie?

① Must
② Would
③ Shall
④ Will
⑤ Won't

14. 다음 대화의 질문에 대한 대답으로 알맞은 것은?

A: Hadn't we better bring some water on our hike?
B: _____

① Yes, we'd better.

② Yes, we better had.

③ Yes, better we had.

④ No, we hadn't better.

⑤ No, we'd not better.

15. 다음 중 밑줄 친 부분을 공통으로 대신할 수 있는 것은?

• <u>Would</u> you please bring me some chopsticks?
• The guests <u>are going to</u> arrive in ten minutes.

① do
② could
③ might
④ will
⑤ may

16. 빈칸에 들어갈 말로 알맞지 <u>않은</u> 것은?

Nancy and I _____ finish our research last night.

① were able to
② weren't able to
③ didn't
④ should
⑤ couldn't

17. 다음 대화의 빈칸에 들어갈 말로 알맞지 <u>않은</u> 것은?

> A: It's so hot! I'd like to go swimming in the river.
> B: You _____ do that. It isn't safe.

① should not
② had better not
③ might not
④ must not
⑤ cannot

18. 다음 중 밑줄 친 부분의 쓰임이 같은 것끼리 묶인 것은?

> a. Spring <u>may</u> come early this year.
> b. Zack <u>may</u> not be able to help us.
> c. Students <u>may</u> not use their notes during tests.
> d. You <u>may</u> not get on a plane without ID.
> e. People <u>may</u> not smoke in office buildings.

① (a, b) – (c, d, e)
② (a, c) – (b, d, e)
③ (a, b, d) – (c, e)
④ (a, c, e) – (b, d)
⑤ (a, b, c) – (d, e)

19. 다음 중 빈칸에 조동사 can이 들어가기에 <u>어색한</u> 것은?
① Stress _____ really hurt your health.
② That _____ be Jared's dad. They look alike.
③ _____ Alison do magic tricks?
④ A problem _____ have many solutions.
⑤ Maria _____ be a little unkind sometimes.

20. 다음 빈칸에 들어갈 말로 알맞게 짝지은 것은?

> Scuba diving is great fun. But before you can go scuba diving, you must take lessons. Then you _____ pass a written test and a swimming test. The swimming test _____ be difficult for some people. You should train for it. You _____ pass the first time, but keep trying!

① must – can – might not
② have to – might – would not
③ must – should – must not
④ should – would – must not
⑤ can – should – might not

21. 다음 문장을 의문문으로 바꿀 때 빈칸에 알맞은 말을 쓰시오. (3점)

> The city would have a festival every summer.

→ _____ every summer?

22. 우리말 의미에 맞도록 문장을 완성하시오. (3점)

> 나는 걸어가야 했기 때문에 학교에 지각했다.

→ I was late for school because I _____ walk.

23. 주어진 단어를 알맞게 배열하여 문장을 완성하시오. (4점)

> A: In your opinion, what might be different in 100 years?
> B: I think people _____ on the moon.

→ _____

(able / be / live / will / to)

24. 다음 대화의 빈칸에 알맞은 말을 순서대로 쓰시오. (4점)

> A: (1) _____ they playing a game now?
> B: The game (2) _____ ended already.

(1) _____

(2) _____

25. 다음 문장에서 어법상 <u>어색한</u> 부분을 찾아 바르게 고쳐 쓰시오. (4점)

> Will Josie or Billy gives the presentation?

→ _____

26. 다음 대화의 빈칸에 알맞은 조동사를 쓰시오. (4점)

> A: I can afford either this jacket or this pair of shorts. What do you think?
> B: You _____ probably buy the shorts since summer is coming.

→ _____

27. 우리말 의미에 맞도록 주어진 단어를 알맞게 배열하시오. (4점)

> 크레이그는 오늘 무엇을 해야 하나요?

→ _____

_____

(does / have / what / today? / do / Craig / to)

28. 두 문장이 같은 뜻이 되도록 빈칸에 알맞은 말을 쓰시오 (4점)

> The librarian couldn't find the book .

→ The librarian _____ to find the book.

29. 우리말 의미에 맞도록 주어진 단어를 알맞게 배열하시오. (5점)

> 그 우유를 냉장고에 넣는 게 좋겠다.

→ _____

_____

(the milk / you / in / had / put / better / the refrigerator)

30. 다음 편지를 읽고 빈칸에 알맞은 조동사를 순서대로 쓰시오. (5점)

> Dear Miss Advice,
> I'm 11, and my older sister (age 15) isn't very nice to me. She (1) _____ let me spend time with her and her friends. What (2) _____ I do?
> Sunny
>
> Dear Sunny,
> Teenagers often don't want to be with younger kids. Try not to worry. In a few years, you and your sister (3) _____ probably be great friends.
> Miss Advice

(1) _____

(2) _____

(3) _____

수동태

Chapter 8 수동태

1 수동태의 쓰임새

주어가 어떤 행위를 하는 것이 아니라 행위의 대상이 되는 문장을 수동태 문장이라고 한다. 수동태 문장의 동사는 〈be 동사 + 타동사의 과거분사〉의 형태이다. 따라서 수동태 문장의 의미상 초점은 행위의 주체가 아니라 행위의 대상 또는 행위 그 자체에 있다. 특히 다음과 같은 경우에는 주로 수동태 문장이 쓰인다.

① 행위자가 아니라 행위 대상을 강조할 때

Grapes **are grown** in the area [by farmers]. (수동)
← Farmers grow grapes in the area. (능동: 행위자에 초점)
I **was born** in 1999.
The mountain **is covered** with snow.

✔ 수동태 문장이 되려면 동사가 목적어를 반드시 필요로 하는 타동사여야 한다. 특히 occur, happen, appear, seem, look, vanish 등과 같은 자동사를 수동태 문장에 쓰지 않도록 주의한다.
Few changes **were occurred** in the region. (X) (occurred로 고쳐야 함)

② 행위자가 누군지 알 수 없을 때

A present **was left** on the teacher's desk.
All the money **was stolen** from my bank account.

③ 행위자를 밝힐 필요가 없거나 밝히고 싶지 않을 때

Wheat **is grown** in the region. (행위자가 농부인 것은 당연하므로)
A mistake **was made**. (행위자에 대한 비난을 피하기 위해)

④ 과학 기술 분야의 글이나 신문 기사에서 격식을 차릴 때

The computer **is protected** from attacks.

Pop Quiz

✎ 괄호 안의 표현 중 알맞은 것을 고르시오.

1. A new airport (completed / was completed) last year.
2. Hackers (are attacking / are attacked) the government's network.
3. English (taught / is taught) in many schools in Korea.
4. All the work (done / is done) on the computer.
5. Fogg (traveled / was traveled) the world in eighty days.

2 수동태 문장 만들기

● **Be 동사 + 타동사의 과거분사**

<u>They</u> <u>cook</u> <u>the food</u> in the kitchen. (능동)

→ The food **is cooked** in the kitchen [by them]. (수동)

　(1) 목적어 the food를 문장 앞으로 보내 주어로 만들고,
　(2) 동사 cook의 시제에 맞게 be 동사의 현재형 is를 쓰고,
　(3) cook의 과거분사형 cooked를 뒤에 추가하고,
　(4) 행위자 및 나머지 요소를 덧붙인다.

My father didn't park the car. (능동)
→ The car **wasn't parked** by my father. (수동)
Our local mailman, Ken, always delivers the mail. (능동)
→ The mail **is always delivered** by our local mailman, Ken. (수동)

Pop Quiz

A. 주어진 동사를 활용하여 수동태 문장을 완성하시오.

1. Many soldiers _____ during the Korean War.　kill

2. A tiger _____ by a boy in the forest yesterday.　see

3. MMORPG games _____ by a large number of teens.　enjoy

4. Spanish _____ in most of South America.　speak

5. The Winter Olympics _____ every four years.　hold

B. 수동태 문장이 되도록 빈칸에 알맞은 말을 쓰시오.

1. Most people hate boring housework.
　→ Boring housework _____ by most people.

2. J. R. R. Tolkien wrote the *Lord of the Rings* books.
　→ The *Lord of the Rings* books _____ by J. R. R. Tolkien.

3. A Chinese company did not make my laptop.
　→ My laptop _____ by a Chinese company.

4. Korean car makers sell millions of cars each year.
　→ Millions of cars _____ each year by Korean car makers.

5. Children around the world send letters to Santa Claus.
　→ Letters _____ to Santa Claus by children around the world.

3 수동태의 시제

Be 동사의 시제를 변환하여 시제를 표현한다.

① 현재: be 동사의 현재형 + 과거분사

The food **is cooked** in the kitchen. (긍정)
The food **is not cooked** in the kitchen. (부정)

② 과거: be 동사의 과거형 + 과거분사

Brazil **was beaten** in the World Cup. (긍정)
Brazil **wasn't beaten** in the World Cup. (부정)

③ 미래: be 동사의 미래형(will be / be going to be) + 과거분사

The project **will be finished** in three days. (긍정)
The project **won't (= will not) be finished** in three days. (부정)
The project **is going to be finished** in three days. (긍정)
The project **isn't (= is not) going to be finished** in three days. (부정)

④ 현재완료: be 동사의 현재완료형(have/has been) + 과거분사

All children **have been given** homework. (긍정)
All children **haven't (= have not) been given** homework. (부정)

⑤ 현재진행 및 과거진행: be 동사의 현재형/과거형 + being + 과거분사

New laws **are being discussed** by the government.
(← The government is discussing new laws.)
New laws **were being discussed** by the government.
(← The government was discussing new laws.)

Pop Quiz

✏️ 주어진 동사를 활용하여 제시된 시제에 맞게 수동태 문장을 완성하시오.

1. [미래 긍정] Balloons _____ away to children under six. give

2. [현재완료 긍정] We _____ to help organize Sports Day. choose

3. [과거 긍정] Barack Obama _____ US president in 2008. elect

4. [과거 부정] The church _____ by Antoni Gaudi. build

5. [현재완료 부정] Cures for some diseases still _____. find

6. [과거 긍정] The dogs _____ to help blind people. train

A. 괄호 안의 표현 중 알맞은 것을 고르시오.

1. Sushi (created / was created) by the Japanese.
2. Cold temperatures and snow (expected / are expected) on Saturday.
3. The thief (has arrested / has been arrested) and put in jail.
4. The fire at our school was probably (started / been started) accidentally.
5. Sungnyemun was (being repaired / been repaired) by skilled builders.

B. 다음 능동태 문장을 수동태 문장으로 바꾸어 쓰시오.

1. The Beatles sang the song "Eight Days a Week."
   → The song "Eight Days a Week" _____.
2. Many companies make tablet computers now.
   → Tablet computers _____ now.
3. My sister rarely beats me when we play table tennis.
   → I _____ when we play table tennis.
4. A famous artist took these beautiful photographs.
   → These beautiful photographs _____.
5. The earthquake destroyed dozens of buildings.
   → Dozens of buildings _____.
6. Millions of Internet users have viewed the video.
   → The video _____.
7. Other people will not read your diary.
   → Your diary _____.
8. The doctor has not examined Michelle yet.
   → Michelle _____ yet.
9. Russia will host the 2018 World Cup.
   → The 2018 World Cup _____.
10. Mr. Yoo was not teaching this history class at this time last year.
    → This history class _____ at this time last year.

C. 우리말 의미에 맞도록 주어진 단어를 활용하여 문장을 완성하시오.

1. These tomatoes _____ by my Mom in her garden. grow
   (이 토마토들은 엄마가 정원에서 재배하는 것들이다.)
2. All of our old clothes _____ to charity. give
   (우리의 모든 낡은 옷은 자선단체에 기증될 것이다.)
3. Violet's room _____ for over a month. clean
   (바이올릿의 방은 한 달 넘도록 청소된 적이 없었다.)
4. Some TV dramas _____ by millions every week. watch
   (일부 텔레비전 드라마는 매주 수백만 명의 사람들이 시청한다.)
5. The telephone _____ by two different men in the same year. invent
   (전화기는 같은 해에 두 사람에 의해서 발명되었다.)

Chapter 8

내신 대비 실전문제

| 이름: | | 시간: 40분 | 점수: | /100 |

선택형 (문항당 3점)

1. 다음 중 수동태 문장은?
   ① I haven't seen Jeff since Monday.
   ② The family was biking by the river.
   ③ Nothing exciting happened yesterday.
   ④ Margaret is standing by the door.
   ⑤ This photo was taken by Greg.

2. 다음 중 주어진 문장과 의미가 비슷한 것은?

   People eat French fries with ketchup.

   ① French fries eat with ketchup.
   ② French fries are eaten with ketchup.
   ③ Ketchup eats with French fries.
   ④ French fries eat with ketchup by people.
   ⑤ People with ketchup eat French fries.

3. 빈칸에 들어갈 말로 알맞은 것은?

   The email was _____ early this morning.

   ① sending   ② send
   ③ sent   ④ to send
   ⑤ sends

4. 두 문장이 같은 뜻이 되도록 할 때 빈칸에 알맞은 말은?

   A friendly old man drives our bus.
   = Our bus _____ driven by a friendly old man.

   ① has   ② have
   ③ are   ④ is
   ⑤ had

5. 다음 중 밑줄 친 부분의 쓰임이 <u>어색한</u> 것은?
   ① Lunch <u>is going to be served</u> soon.
   ② Lena <u>was seemed</u> happy with her gift.
   ③ Several languages <u>are spoken</u> in Switzerland.
   ④ The winner <u>won't be chosen</u> until next week.
   ⑤ The hackers <u>were caught</u> by the police.

6. 두 문장이 같은 뜻이 되도록 할 때 빈칸에 알맞은 말은?

   The whole school will see the play.
   = The play will _____ by the whole school.

   ① be seen   ② have seen
   ③ be saw   ④ be see
   ⑤ see

7. 다음 문장의 밑줄 친 단어를 옳게 고쳐 쓴 것은?

   Has the dog <u>was</u> taken outside yet today?

   ① being   ② has
   ③ be   ④ have
   ⑤ been

8. 우리말 의미에 맞도록 할 때 빈칸에 알맞은 말은?

   미첼은 1995년에 런던에서 태어났다.
   = Mitchell _____ in London in 1995.

   ① born   ② has born
   ③ is born   ④ being born
   ⑤ was born

9. 다음 중 어법상 <u>어색한</u> 것은?
   ① Lawyers in Korea study for six years.
   ② *Avatar* was directed by James Cameron.
   ③ Cherie looks very nice in that dress.
   ④ Was everyone shocked by the bad news?
   ⑤ Smart phones often used for email.

10. 우리말 의미에 맞도록 할 때 빈칸에 알맞은 말은?

    시내에 새 호텔이 완공되었다.
    = A new hotel _____ built downtown.

    ① has been
    ② was been
    ③ have been
    ④ has be
    ⑤ was be

11. 두 문장이 같은 뜻이 되도록 할 때 빈칸에 알맞은 말은?

    Nathan answered all my questions.
    = All my questions were _____ by Nathan.

    ① answer
    ② answered
    ③ answering
    ④ answers
    ⑤ to answer

12. 다음 중 밑줄 친 부분의 쓰임이 <u>어색한</u> 것은?
    ① Egypt <u>is knew</u> for its amazing pyramids.
    ② The classroom <u>is cleaned</u> once a week.
    ③ This rice <u>hasn't been cooked</u> yet.
    ④ The big storm <u>wasn't expected</u>.
    ⑤ The light bulb <u>was invented</u> by Edison.

13. 우리말 의미에 맞도록 밑줄 친 단어를 옳게 고쳐 쓴 것은?

    야구 시합이 아마도 취소될 것이다.
    = The baseball game is probably going to <u>cancel</u>.

    ① canceled
    ② is canceled
    ③ be canceled
    ④ be canceling
    ⑤ canceling

14. 다음 대화의 빈칸에 들어갈 말로 알맞은 것은?

    A: That used car looks new.
    B: Yes, it _____ been driven very much.

    ① aren't
    ② was
    ③ won't
    ④ hasn't
    ⑤ doesn't

15. 다음 중 밑줄 친 단어를 옳게 고쳐 쓴 것은?

    The cake had already been <u>cutting</u> into six pieces.

    ① cut
    ② cuts
    ③ to cut
    ④ was cut
    ⑤ cutted

16. 다음 빈칸에 공통으로 들어갈 말로 알맞은 것은?

    • Tom and Diana _____ married for ten years.
    • I want to sit down, but all the seats _____ taken.

    ① were being
    ② have been
    ③ being
    ④ have
    ⑤ is

17. 다음 빈칸에 들어갈 말로 알맞게 짝지은 것은?

> • This website _____ by thousands of people every day.
> • I'm _____ my friend at the hospital.

① visited – visiting
② is visited – being visited
③ is visited – visiting
④ visits – being visited
⑤ visits – visited

18. 다음 중 밑줄 친 부분의 쓰임이 옳은 것은?

① Many accidents <u>are occurred</u> on the highway.
② Some money <u>was took</u> from Jen's bag.
③ Several students <u>will be give</u> awards.
④ The message <u>was written</u> in English.
⑤ Your computer <u>hasn't fixed</u> yet.

19. 다음 빈칸에 들어갈 말로 알맞게 짝지은 것은?

> • I _____ the piece of paper in half.
> • The piece of paper has _____ in half.
> • The piece of paper _____ in half.

① torn – been torn – torn
② tore – torn – was torn
③ tore – been torn – was torn
④ was torn – tore – has torn
⑤ was torn – torn – torn

20. 우리말 의미에 맞도록 주어진 단어를 알맞게 배열한 것은?

> 실내화는 대개 집에서 신는다.
> = _____
> (at home / worn / slippers / usually / are)

① Slippers are usually worn at home.
② Usually are slippers worn at home.
③ Slippers are at home worn usually.
④ At home are slippers usually worn.
⑤ At home usually worn are slippers.

21. 우리말 의미에 맞도록 문장을 완성하시오. (3점)

> 최종 결정은 아직 내려지지 않았다.

→ The final decision has _____ yet.

22. 우리말 의미에 맞도록 문장을 완성하시오. (3점)

> 이번 주 컴퓨터 동호회 모임은 목요일 오후 3시에 열릴 것입니다.

→ This week's computer club meeting

_____ on Thursday at 3 p.m.

23. 다음 밑줄 친 단어를 바르게 고쳐 쓰시오. (4점)

> <u>Have</u> you woken up by the loud music last night?

→ _____

24. 다음 중 밑줄 친 동사의 형태가 <u>어색한</u> 것을 골라 바르게 고쳐 쓰시오. (4점)

> The *Mona Lisa* ① <u>has been studied</u> more than any other painting. This famous picture ② <u>was painted</u> by Leonardo da Vinci in the early 1500s, and it ③ <u>shows</u> a woman with an unusual smile. It has been in the Louvre Museum in Paris for many years. In 1911, the *Mona Lisa* ④ <u>stole</u> from the Louvre. Luckily, it ⑤ <u>was found</u> two years later.

_____ → _____

25. 다음 밑줄 친 부분을 바르게 고쳐 쓰시오. (4점)

> A bear <u>haven't be</u> seen in that forest since I came here six years ago.

→ _____

26. 두 문장이 같은 뜻이 되도록 빈칸에 알맞은 말을 쓰시오. (4점)

My mom grows these pretty flowers.

→ These pretty flowers _____

_____.

27. 다음 문장에서 어법상 <u>어색한</u> 부분을 찾아 바르게 고쳐 쓰시오. (4점)

> Kim and Joseph aren't going to invited to the party.

→ _____

_____

28. 주어진 단어를 알맞게 배열하여 문장을 완성하시오. (4점)

> have   concert tickets   all the   sold   been

→ _____

29. 다음 문장을 능동태로 바꾸어 쓰시오. (5점)

> The basement was being used as a workshop by a local artist.

→ _____

_____

30. 다음 글을 읽고 주어진 단어를 알맞게 배열하여 문장을 완성하시오. (5점)

> Ladies and gentlemen, welcome to Incheon International Airport. This is an announcement about flight 674 to Hong Kong. The (delayed / by / flight / been / bad weather / has). It will be about one hour late and will take off at 4:30 p.m. We are sorry for the delay. Thank you.

→ The _____

_____.

To Be or Not to Be; That is the Question.

부정사

부정사

1 명사 역할을 하는 To 부정사

〈to + 동사원형〉의 형태로 동사의 성격을 그대로 가지면서 문장 내에서 주어, 목적어, 보어 등 명사가 하는 역할을 한다.

1 주어 역할을 하는 **To 부정사**: to 부정사구가 짧은 경우에 사용하며, 형식적인 느낌을 준다.

To see is to believe.
To be kind to others is important.

- to 부정사구가 길 때는 가주어 it을 사용하여 문장을 시작하고 to 부정사구를 문장의 끝에 둔다.
  It is important **to eat healthy food**.
  (← To eat healthy food is important.)
  It is unusual **to see an owl during the day**.
  (← To see an owl during the day is unusual.)

2 목적어 역할을 하는 **To 부정사**: 목적어로 주로 to 부정사를 취하는 동사들이 있다.

want, hope, wish, ask, decide, plan, expect, promise, agree, refuse, . . .

Tom **wants to attend** the Massachusetts Institute of Technology.
Many people **wish to make** the environment better.
John **decided to get up** early.

- to 부정사 앞에 not을 붙여 부정형을 만든다.
  Marcus promised **not to throw** stones at the birds.

3 주격보어 역할을 하는 **To 부정사**

My homework is **to send** an email to my grandparents.
Tony's hope is **to visit** New York.

Pop Quiz

 알맞은 단어를 골라 to 부정사의 형태로 쓰시오.

stay	work	pay	visit	finish	be	become

1. Harry wants _____ Korea for his next vacation.

2. It was difficult _____ reading this long, boring book.

3. _____ healthier is also to be happier.

4. June and I plan _____ harder in school next semester.

5. It is expensive _____ at a 5-star hotel.

6. Andrea's dream is _____ an animal doctor someday.

7. The man refused _____ for his meal because it tasted terrible.

2 형용사 역할을 하는 To 부정사 —————

명사나 대명사 뒤에서 그 명사나 대명사를 꾸며주는 역할을 하며, "~할"이라는 의미로 쓰인다.

❶ 명사 수식

Daniel has a lot of **homework to do**.
What is the best **way to hunt** rabbits?
My mom always says that she has no **time to exercise**.

❷ 대명사 수식

Would you like **something to drink**?
There's **nothing to hide** between my sister and me.
Emily doesn't have **anyone to chat with**. (anyone은 chat with의 목적어)

• 대명사 뒤에 수식하는 형용사가 이미 있는 경우 to 부정사는 그 형용사 뒤에 위치한다.
  Do you have **something cold to drink**?
  I'm looking for **something new to read** in this newspaper.

❸ It's (about) time + to 부정사: "~할 시간이다"

It's time to dance.
It's time to say goodbye to yesterday.
I think **it's about time to close** the shop and go home.

Pop Quiz

🖉 주어진 단어를 알맞게 배열하여 문장을 완성하시오.

1. The professor gave each student _____.
   (topic / research / different / to / a)

2. I can't find _____.
   (to / watch / good / anything / on TV)

3. Eating an apple is an _____.
   (important / way / to / easy / vitamins / get)

4. Greg isn't feeling well, but I'm sure it is _____.
   (worry / about / to / nothing)

5. The weather is getting cold, so it's _____.
   (turn on / to / heater / about / the / time)

6. Serena rarely has _____.
   (see / her / chance / a / cousins / to)

7. Jason complains that he doesn't have _____.
   (free / his / anything / time / do /in / to)

3 부사 역할을 하는 To 부정사

형용사, 동사, 부사를 수식하는 역할을 한다.

1 형용사를 꾸며주는 역할 (〜하기에)

Love is sometimes **hard to understand**.
I'm not **ready to go** to college yet.
Some people are **easy to please**.

2 동사의 목적을 설명해 주는 역할 (〜하기 위해서)

Peter wanted to go to Paris **to study** art.
A frog uses its long tongue **to catch** food.

3 감정의 원인을 나타내는 역할 (〜해서)

I'm so happy **to have** you as my friend.
My mom was disappointed **to see** my math score.

4 결과를 나타내는 역할 (〜하게 되다)

My grandfather lived **to be** 90 years old.
My cousin grew up **to be** a pianist.

4 원형부정사

원형부정사는 종종 동사원형이라 불리며, 사역동사 또는 지각동사의 목적격보어로 쓰인다.

1 사역동사(**make/have/let**) + 목적어 + 원형부정사

My mom let me **go** to an amusement park with my friends.
Andy made his son **keep** a diary every day.

2 지각동사(**see, watch, hear, listen to, feel**) + 목적어 + 원형부정사

Russell watched his sons **play** basketball.
Linda heard her daughter **play** the flute.

Pop Quiz

 괄호 안의 표현 중 알맞은 것을 고르시오.

1. This river is dangerous (swim / to swim) in.

2. Did anyone see that man (steal / to steal) my bike?

3. At his party, Jamie had his guests (play / to play) some silly games.

4. The team was thrilled (score / to score) its first goal of the season.

5. Seoul has grown (be / to be) one of the world's biggest cities.

6. You must brush your teeth at least twice a day (keep / to keep) them healthy.

7. I like listening to the rain (fall / to fall) on the roof.

8. The doctor made the man (start / to start) exercising.

9. For me, math is difficult (understand / to understand).

10. I bought this vase (give / to give) to my grandmother on her birthday.

A. 주어진 단어를 알맞은 형태로 바꾸어 쓰시오.

1. I never agree _____ my friends to use my cell phone. (allow)
2. Our parents let us _____ out until 11 p.m. (stay)
3. The couple is planning _____ married in the spring. (get)
4. The purpose of lifting weights is _____ strong muscles. (build)
5. Everyone felt the floor _____ during the earthquake. (shake)

B. 주어진 단어들을 알맞게 배열하여 문장을 완성하시오.

1. Dana (tell / decided / to / everyone) the truth.
   → _____

2. What is the (way / fastest / get / to) downtown?
   → _____

3. We all felt very (to / see / relieved / plane / the) land safely.
   → _____

4. (rude / is / it / to / chew) food with your mouth open.
   → _____

5. Let's think of (fun / to / something / do) this weekend.
   → _____

C. 괄호 안의 표현 중 알맞은 것을 고르시오.

1. My mother promised (buying / to buy) me new shoes for my birthday.
2. Do your teachers make you (give / to give) many presentations?
3. Our plan is (finish / to finish) the project by the end of the month.
4. Terry doesn't let anyone (say / to say) bad things about his sister.
5. It's interesting (see / to see) old photos of ourselves.

D. 우리말 의미에 맞도록 문장을 완성하시오.

1. It _____ a new language.
   (새로운 언어를 배우는 데는 시간이 많이 걸린다.)

2. The two brothers _____ anymore.
   (두 형제는 더는 싸우지 않는 데에 동의했다.)

3. We have only _____.
   (우리는 시험 하나만 더 보면 된다.)

4. I'm always glad _____.
   (나는 언제나 새로운 친구를 사귀는 게 즐겁다.)

5. In the future, more people will _____.
   (미래에는 더욱 많은 사람이 100세까지 살 수 있을 것이다.)

내신 대비 실전문제

이름: | 시간: 40분 | 점수: /100

선택형 (문항당 3점)

1. 빈칸에 들어갈 말로 알맞은 것은?

> Everyone needs _____ alone sometimes.

① be   ② is
③ to be   ④ are
⑤ being

2. 다음 중 밑줄 친 부분의 쓰임이 어색한 것은?

> ① <u>Nancy's goal</u> ② <u>is</u> ③ <u>write</u> ④ <u>a book</u> ⑤ <u>about</u> her family.

①   ②   ③   ④   ⑤

3. 다음 중 밑줄 친 부분의 쓰임이 <u>다른</u> 하나는?
① We need someone older <u>to talk</u> to.
② The baby needs something <u>to eat</u>.
③ Is there anywhere comfortable <u>to sit</u>?
④ The music was difficult <u>to hear</u>.
⑤ Ken has nothing <u>to do</u> tonight.

4. 다음 문장의 밑줄 친 부분과 쓰임이 <u>다른</u> 하나는?

> It's easy <u>to find</u> the children's park.

① It was nice <u>to see</u> Mr. Lim.
② It will be hard <u>to get</u> a taxi.
③ It is scary <u>to fly</u> in a small plane.
④ It is time <u>to leave</u> for school.
⑤ It was fun <u>to swim</u> in the lake.

5. 우리말 의미에 맞도록 주어진 단어를 알맞게 배열한 것은?

> 새 유니폼을 사야 할 때가 거의 됐어.
> = It's (to / new / buy / about / uniforms / time).

① It's about time to new uniforms buy.
② It's time about to buy new uniforms.
③ It's about time new uniforms to buy.
④ It's to buy about time new uniforms.
⑤ It's about time to buy new uniforms.

6. 다음 문장의 밑줄 친 부분과 쓰임이 <u>다른</u> 하나는?

> Mike's idea was <u>to get</u> a part-time job.

① The purpose of the book is <u>to teach</u> photography.
② The computer started <u>to make</u> strange noises.
③ Tina's plan was <u>to study</u> abroad.
④ My hobby was <u>to read</u> mystery novels.
⑤ One way to save money is <u>to eat</u> at home.

7. 다음 중 어법상 <u>어색한</u> 것은?
① Make mistakes is human.
② Choose a chair and sit down.
③ Remember to bring your passport.
④ Read the instructions first.
⑤ Take off your shoes when you enter.

8. 다음 중 밑줄 친 부분의 쓰임이 <u>다른</u> 하나는?
① There's no reason <u>to cry</u> about it.
② We have so many dishes <u>to wash</u>!
③ Nora doesn't have any money <u>to spend</u>.
④ Did you have a chance <u>to talk</u> to Mary?
⑤ Don't forget <u>to pay</u> the bill.

9. 다음 중 밑줄 친 부분의 쓰임이 <u>다른</u> 하나는?
   ① Are the cookies ready <u>to eat</u>?
   ② Was your dog easy <u>to train</u>?
   ③ The problem was difficult <u>to solve</u>.
   ④ The doctor gave him medicine <u>to take</u>.
   ⑤ Her accent is hard <u>to understand</u>.

10. 우리말 의미에 맞도록 주어진 단어를 알맞게 배열한 것은?

    우리는 이야기를 나눌 수 있는 조용한 곳이 필요해.
    = We need (quiet / to / somewhere / chat).

    ① We need quiet somewhere to chat.
    ② We need somewhere quiet to chat.
    ③ We need to chat quiet somewhere.
    ④ We need quiet to chat somewhere.
    ⑤ We need to somewhere quiet chat.

11. 다음 문장의 밑줄 친 부분과 쓰임이 <u>다른</u> 하나는?

    Carla wants <u>to sit</u> with us.

    ① The cat refused <u>to eat</u> its dinner.
    ② Are you planning <u>to walk</u> home?
    ③ Bill might decide <u>to help</u> us.
    ④ Why did Elly turn around <u>to look</u> at me?
    ⑤ I don't expect <u>to have</u> free time.

12. 다음 문장의 밑줄 친 부분과 쓰임이 같은 것은?

    Is your sister glad <u>to be</u> home from college?

    ① The fans were excited <u>to watch</u> the game.
    ② Take an extra sweater <u>to stay</u> warm.
    ③ We helped Eric <u>to find</u> his keys.
    ④ Is this water safe <u>to drink</u>?
    ⑤ It's necessary <u>to check</u> your computer for viruses.

13. 빈칸에 들어갈 말로 알맞은 것은?

    We will have an important decision _____ tomorrow.

    ① make   ② to make
    ③ making   ④ made
    ⑤ makes

14. 다음 문장의 밑줄 친 부분과 쓰임이 같은 것은?

    Steve called me <u>to ask</u> about you.

    ① Everyone was sorry <u>to hear</u> the sad news.
    ② Jenna chooses great movies <u>to watch</u>.
    ③ Do you need something <u>to write</u> with?
    ④ This floor is hard <u>to clean</u>.
    ⑤ I went outside <u>to get</u> some fresh air.

15. 빈칸에 들어갈 말로 알맞은 것은?

    The kids threw a party _____ Jim's birthday.

    ① celebrate   ② are celebrating
    ③ celebrates   ④ celebrated
    ⑤ to celebrate

16. 다음 중 빈칸에 "to"가 들어갈 수 있는 것은?
    ① Dad makes my brother _____ eat his dinner.
    ② The actress hoped _____ become famous.
    ③ Jill doesn't let anyone _____ borrow money.
    ④ I enjoy watching the clouds _____ go by.
    ⑤ Kevin saw you _____ walk into class.

17. 다음 문장의 밑줄 친 부분과 쓰임이 같은 것은?

The circus is very exciting to watch.

① It's unhealthy to eat too much sugar.
② They're looking for an apartment to rent.
③ Lisa loves to do crossword puzzles.
④ Her ideas were simple to understand.
⑤ I'm surprised to see Jason here.

18. 다음 빈칸에 들어갈 말로 알맞게 짝지은 것은?

• Mom doesn't allow me _____ TV late at night.
• Listen to those birds _____!

① to watch – sing
② to watch – to sing
③ watch – singing
④ to watching – singing
⑤ watching – to sing

19. 다음 중 밑줄 친 부분의 쓰임이 옳은 것은?
① Laura went to the theater see a play.
② I was angry see the big mess.
③ She felt someone touch her hand.
④ They never learned play an instrument.
⑤ It isn't unusual get a cold in winter.

20. 다음 중 어법상 어색한 것은?

① I had ② an artist ③ to paint ④ a picture ⑤ for me.

①   ②   ③   ④   ⑤

21. 주어진 단어를 알맞게 배열하여 문장을 완성하시오. (3점)

buy   to   a new   not   car

→ My parents decided _____.

22. 우리말 의미에 맞도록 주어진 단어를 알맞게 배열하여 문장을 완성하시오. (3점)

마리아는 성적을 향상시킬 방법을 찾아야 해.

→ Maria must find _____.
(improve / her / to / grades / a / way)

23. 다음 중 어법상 어색한 문장을 골라 바르게 고쳐 쓰시오. (4점)

① I hate ride on a crowded subway.
② Ben doesn't like to sing.
③ Michelle didn't hear the bell ring.
④ The principal let us go home early.
⑤ We tried to stay awake until midnight.

→ _____

24. 두 문장이 같은 뜻이 되도록 to 부정사를 사용하여 문장을 완성하시오. (4점)

You should say *thank you*. It's polite.

→ It's polite _____.

25. 두 문장이 같은 뜻이 되도록 밑줄 친 단어를 알맞은 부정사의 형태로 바꾸어 쓰시오. (4점)

Tom cannot join the baseball team.

→ Tom's parents won't allow him _____ the baseball team.

26. 다음 문장에서 어법상 <u>어색한</u> 부분을 찾아 바르게 고쳐 쓰시오. (4점)

> Roberta promised to be not late for practice.

→ _____

27. 우리말 의미에 맞도록 문장을 완성하시오. (4점)

> 쉬려면 네 침대에 가서 누워라.

→ Lie down on your bed _____.

28. 주어진 단어를 알맞게 배열하여 문장을 완성하시오. (4점)

> to   decision   a   motorcycle   buy

→ Michael has made a _____

_____.

고난도 서술형

29. 우리말 의미에 맞도록 문장을 완성하시오. (5점)

> 패트릭은 입을 새 옷이 필요하다.

→ Patrick needs _____

_____.

30. 다음 그림과 설명을 보고 주어진 단어를 사용하여 이야기를 완성하시오. (5점)

Lori and Mark went to a theater to watch a movie. A man sat in front of them.
He began to talk loudly on his cell phone.
So _____

_____. (asked, be, quiet)

Flying is definitely not as dangerous as riding a bike.

Quattro
Grammar
Start

동명사

10 동명사

1 동명사의 역할

동명사는 〈동사원형 + -ing〉의 형태로 문장의 주어, 보어, 목적어 등 명사의 역할을 한다. 또한 동사의 성질을 갖고 있기 때문에 목적어를 동반할 수 있다.

① 주어 역할

Learning is the way to a better future.
Studying after the test is not useful.
Keeping pets is good for children. (목적어 동반)

② 보어 역할

My job is **teaching** music.
Cosette's wish was **seeing** her father again.
John's dream is **traveling** around the world.

③ 목적어 역할

1> 타동사의 목적어: finish, enjoy, mind, avoid, quit, give up, deny 등의 타동사는 동명사를 목적어로 취한다.
Many people don't enjoy **eating** alone.
Mike stopped **watching** TV and went out for a walk.
When I finished **washing** my car, it began to rain.

2> 전치사의 목적어: 전치사 뒤에는 기본적으로 명사를 써야 하지만, 의미상 행위를 나타내는 표현을 써야 할 때는 동명사를 쓴다.
Janice is very good **at playing** the guitar.
I am really afraid **of swimming** in the ocean.
By taking a taxi to go to the ballpark, we can save time.

Pop Quiz

 빈칸에 알맞은 단어를 골라 알맞은 형태로 문장을 완성하시오.

make	play	read	collect	invite	see	choose

1. I don't like skiing, but I really enjoy _____ ice hockey.

2. _____ pizza requires an oven.

3. Rick is excited about _____ his old friend again.

4. The first step in writing an essay is _____ a topic.

5. _____ Pokemon cards used to be very popular.

6. Are you planning on _____ Debra to dinner?

7. Because of the Internet, many people have stopped _____ newspapers.

2 동명사와 현재분사

동명사와 현재분사는 둘 다 〈동사원형 + -ing〉의 형태이지만, 동명사는 명사의 역할을 하고 현재분사는 형용사의 역할을 한다는 점에서 다르다.

Does the White House have a **swimming** pool? (동명사)
Wow! Look at that **swimming** baby. (명사를 수식하는 현재분사)
That 14-day-old baby is **swimming** in the pool. (현재진행형을 만드는 현재분사)
By taking **singing** lessons online, you can learn how to sing. (동명사)
Can you see that **singing** bird in the tree? (명사를 수식하는 현재분사)

3 동명사와 To 부정사

동명사를 목적어로 취하는 동사	finish, enjoy, mind, avoid, quit, give up, deny, . . .
To 부정사를 목적어로 취하는 동사	want, hope, decide, plan, wish, expect, . . .
둘 다 목적어로 취하는 동사	like, hate, love, begin, start, continue, . . .
목적어에 따라 의미가 달라지는 동사	forget, remember, try, stop, regret, . . .

• 동명사를 목적어로 취하는 동사에는 대개 일반적인 행위 및 과거와 관련된 행위를 나타내는 동사들이 포함되며, to 부정사를 목적어로 취하는 동사에는 구체적인 행위 및 미래와 관련된 행위를 나타내는 동사들이 포함된다. 둘 다 목적어로 취하는 동사의 경우에도 이런 의미 차이가 적용된다.

The girl **plans to go** to the park.
I **remember meeting** him before, but I don't know his name.
I **forgot to tell** my students that we don't have exams tomorrow. ("말해야 할 것을 잊었다")
I **forgot telling** my students that we don't have exams tomorrow. ("말해 놓고 잊었다")

Pop Quiz

A. 밑줄 친 단어가 동명사인지 현재분사인지 쓰시오.

1. Chile is famous for <u>producing</u> wine. (   )
2. The police officer stopped the <u>speeding</u> car. (   )
3. I found the instructions for my printer very <u>confusing</u>. (   )
4. Gail's least favorite chore is <u>doing</u> laundry. (   )

B. 괄호 안의 표현 중 알맞은 것을 고르시오.

1. Nora wants (living / to live) in Hawaii in the winter.
2. Avoid (to drink / drinking) coffee or tea before bed.
3. If you wish (joining / to join) the computer club, come to room 201.
4. I remember (taking / to take) long walks with my dad as a kid.

4 동명사의 관용적 표현

1 Go + -ing: "~하러 가다"

I want to **go camping** with my friends this summer.
Let's **go surfing** this weekend.
Christine **went shopping** and bought a pair of jeans for her daughter.

2 How/What about + -ing?: "~하는 게 어때?"

What about playing basketball after school?
Mom, **how about eating** out tonight?

3 Spend time + -ing: "~데 시간을 보내다"

My son **spends** more **time watching** TV than at school.
Fidel **spends** too much **time playing** mobile games.

4 Cannot/Can't help + -ing: "~하지 않을 수 없다"

I just **can't help thinking** of my lost dog.
Jimmy **couldn't help laughing** when his mother yelled at his brother.

5 It's no use + -ing: "~해도 소용없다"

It's no use going back to yesterday.
It's no use crying over spilt milk.

6 Look forward to + -ing: "~하기를 고대하다"

I'm **looking forward to hearing** from you soon.
Derek **is looking forward to meeting** Jim's new girlfriend.

7 Have difficulty/trouble/fun + -ing: "~하는 데 어려움/곤란/재미를 느끼다"

I **have difficulty getting** a part-time job.
My dog **had fun chasing** grasshoppers at the park.

Pop Quiz

✎ 괄호 안의 표현 중 알맞은 것을 고르시오.

1. Eric (had trouble / couldn't help) getting home during the snowstorm.

2. Before a big exam, I (look forward to / spend a lot of time) reviewing my notes.

3. If you're bored, (go / how about) hiking with us in the forest?

4. (It's no use / I'm looking forward to) spending money on low-quality clothes.

5. Parents (can't help / have fun) worrying about their children.

6. (It's no use / I look forward to) decorating my new bedroom.

7. Stephanie (can't help / goes) scuba diving every summer.

Grammar Practice

A. 주어진 단어를 알맞은 형태로 바꾸어 쓰시오.

1. Thank you for _____ to my story. `listen`
2. Downloading music without _____ for it is against the law. `pay`
3. _____ is a way for many animals to get food. `hunt`
4. You can become a happier person by _____ others. `help`
5. Joan doesn't mind _____ early in the morning. `wake up`

B. 괄호 안의 표현 중 알맞은 것을 고르시오.

1. I am interested (in collecting / to collect) old stamps.
2. Peter decided (joining / to join) the army after high school.
3. How about (to take / taking) a short break now?
4. There's no soda because I forgot (buying / to buy) some.
5. My brother is really good at (to fix / fixing) bikes.

C. 다음 밑줄 친 부분을 바르게 고쳐 쓰시오.

1. John loves <u>swim</u>, but he hates to jump into cold water. → _____
2. Please remember <u>turning off</u> the TV before going out. → _____
3. Do Korean students enjoy <u>to speak</u> English with native speakers? → _____
4. I want to thank Valerie for <u>lend</u> me her camera. → _____
5. Everyone's looking forward to <u>attend</u> the school festival. → _____

D. 우리말 의미에 맞도록 문장을 완성하시오.

1. What about _____ this Saturday?
   (이번 토요일에 낚시하러 가는 거 어때요?)

2. _____ makes your skin healthier.
   (물 마시는 것은 네 피부를 건강하게 해 준다.)

3. My best friend spends _____.
   (내 친구는 운동하는 데에 많은 시간을 쓴다.)

4. Wendy is afraid of _____.
   (웬디는 감기 걸리는 것을 두려워한다.)

5. We are going to _____ this entire book.
   (우리는 이 책을 다 읽는 데 어려움이 있을 것이다.)

선택형 (문항당 3점)

1. 다음 중 밑줄 친 단어를 옳게 고쳐 쓴 것은?

> <u>Give</u> tests is part of teaching.

① Gives   ② Given

③ Gave   ④ Giving

⑤ Give

2. 우리말 의미에 맞도록 할 때 빈칸에 알맞은 말은?

> 나는 이름을 정말 잘 외우지 못한다.
> = I'm really bad at _____ names.

① remember   ② remembering

③ to remember   ④ remembered

⑤ remembers

3. 다음 중 밑줄 친 부분의 쓰임이 옳은 것은?

① Hanna hates <u>spending</u> money.

② I forgot <u>tell</u> you the news.

③ The cats enjoy <u>to drink</u> milk.

④ Do you want <u>going</u> to sleep?

⑤ Let's finish <u>to eat</u> lunch.

4. 다음 중 밑줄 친 부분의 쓰임이 <u>다른</u> 하나는?

① Kevin's job was <u>delivering</u> pizza.

② The next step is <u>cutting</u> the vegetables.

③ The boys continued <u>playing</u> all day.

④ Molly's hobby was <u>making</u> dolls.

⑤ His dream is <u>sailing</u> around the world.

5. 다음 대화의 빈칸에 들어갈 말로 알맞은 것은?

> A: Why did it take you an hour to get home?
> B: We stopped _____ lunch.

① having   ② have

③ to have   ④ had

⑤ has

6. 다음 중 밑줄 친 부분의 쓰임이 <u>어색한</u> 것은?

① Troy doesn't let me <u>wear</u> his jacket.

② Jane practices <u>hit</u> a baseball.

③ The teacher made us <u>sit</u> down.

④ I'd like to <u>take</u> singing lessons.

⑤ Help them <u>clean</u> the living room.

7. 다음 빈칸에 들어갈 말로 알맞게 짝지은 것은?

> • Do you expect _____ a present?
> • It started _____ ten minutes ago.

① to get – raining

② get – raining

③ getting – to rain

④ getting – rain

⑤ to get – rain

8. 다음 중 밑줄 친 부분의 쓰임이 <u>어색한</u> 것은?

① You'll make more friends by <u>be</u> nice.

② Is <u>drinking</u> coffee bad for you?

③ Lisa had me <u>cut</u> her hair.

④ Do you <u>know</u> Brad's family name?

⑤ <u>Doing</u> puzzles is a lot of fun.

9. 다음 문장의 밑줄 친 부분과 쓰임이 같은 것은?

> Carrie helps the <u>crying</u> child.

① <u>Scoring</u> a goal in soccer is hard.
② Hikers must watch for <u>falling</u> rocks.
③ I know little about <u>designing</u> websites.
④ She doesn't remember <u>saying</u> that.
⑤ Please stop <u>talking</u> now.

10. 다음 빈칸에 들어갈 말로 알맞게 짝지은 것은?

> • Don't forget _____ me tomorrow.
> • _____ to your parents is wrong.

① meeting – Lying
② to meet – Lie
③ meet – Lie
④ meeting – To lie
⑤ to meet – Lying

11. 빈칸에 들어갈 말로 알맞은 것은?

> I regret _____ poorly in yesterday's race.

① to do   ② do
③ doing   ④ does
⑤ did

12. 다음 문장의 밑줄 친 부분과 쓰임이 같은 것은?

> <u>Exercising</u> every day is important.

① The <u>barking</u> dogs woke me up.
② <u>Growing</u> children need good food.
③ The burning <u>building</u> was empty.
④ <u>Taking</u> long showers wastes water.
⑤ <u>Rising</u> prices make shoppers unhappy.

13. 다음 빈칸에 들어갈 말로 알맞게 짝지은 것은?

> • Richard stopped _____ for his health.
> • This book is about _____ a career.

① smoke – to choose
② to smoke – choosing
③ smoking – choosing
④ smoking – to choose
⑤ to smoke – to choose

14. 다음 문장의 밑줄 친 부분과 쓰임이 같은 것은?

> Everyone was <u>sleeping</u> at 11 p.m.

① Jason's goal is <u>becoming</u> a singer.
② Valerie is <u>taking</u> the subway to the mall.
③ One bad habit is <u>biting</u> your nails.
④ Our first task was <u>making</u> a shopping list.
⑤ My favorite thing about summer is <u>swimming</u>.

15. 다음 대화의 밑줄 친 부분 중 어법상 옳은 것은?

> A: Do you often ① <u>going</u> to the movies, Alison?
> B: No, I like ② <u>watching</u> movies at home.
> A: Really? I think ③ <u>see</u> them at the theater is more fun.
> B: Yes, it's nice ④ <u>see</u> them on a big screen. But I hate ⑤ <u>pay</u> for a ticket.

①   ②   ③   ④   ⑤

16. 다음 중 밑줄 친 부분의 쓰임이 다른 하나는?

① Peter loves <u>doing</u> math.
② They discussed <u>canceling</u> the picnic.
③ I don't mind <u>walking</u> home.
④ Mom likes <u>sleeping</u> late.
⑤ We talked about <u>joining</u> a club.

17. 우리말 의미에 맞도록 주어진 단어를 알맞게 배열한 것은?

> 마크는 책 읽는 데 많은 시간을 쓰지 않는다.
> = Mark doesn't (much / reading / spend / time / books).

① Mark doesn't reading books much time spend.
② Mark doesn't much time spend books reading.
③ Mark doesn't spend much time reading books.
④ Mark doesn't spend much time books reading.
⑤ Mark doesn't spend time much reading books.

18. 다음 대화의 빈칸에 들어갈 말로 알맞은 것은?

> A: I emailed you my essay. Did you read it?
> B: No, I had trouble _____ the file.

① opening   ② open
③ opened   ④ to open
⑤ opens

19. 다음 중 밑줄 친 동사의 형태가 어법상 어색한 것은?

> My parents make me ① watch my little brother every afternoon. I don't mind ② to do it. We have fun ③ playing games. I also like ④ to teach him new things. Tomorrow I'll begin ⑤ teaching him to ride a bike.

①   ②   ③   ④   ⑤

20. 다음 빈칸에 들어갈 말로 알맞게 짝지은 것은?

> • I'm looking forward to _____ a new school year.
> • Can we go _____ tonight?

① start – dancing
② starting – to dance
③ to start – dance
④ starting – dancing
⑤ start – to dance

서술형

21. 다음 대화의 빈칸에 들어갈 알맞은 말을 쓰시오. (3점)

> A: I have a terrible headache.
> B: Try _____ some aspirin.

→ _____

22. 우리말 의미에 맞도록 주어진 단어를 알맞게 배열하여 문장을 완성하시오. (3점)

> 댄은 연설 중에 잠이 드는 것을 참을 수가 없었다.

→ Dan _____
during the speech.
(help / asleep / falling / couldn't)

23. 다음 중 밑줄 친 부분의 쓰임이 어색한 것을 골라 바르게 고쳐 쓰시오. (4점)

> ① Beautiful music began to play.
> ② They hate to miss their favorite TV show.
> ③ It's no use trying to explain.
> ④ How about to go fishing this weekend?
> ⑤ Marie is afraid of touching a spider.

→ _____

24. 우리말 의미에 맞도록 문장을 완성하시오. (4점)

> 쉴라는 큰 집에서 사는 꿈을 꾼다.

→ Sheila dreams of _____
in a big house.

25. 다음 문장에서 어법상 <u>어색한</u> 부분을 찾아 바르게 고쳐 쓰시오. (4점)

> The dog has difficulty to walk on two legs.

→ _____

26. 괄호 안의 표현 중 알맞은 것을 골라 순서대로 쓰시오. (4점)

> (1) (Taking / Take) public transportation is a good idea. Subways and buses are fast and convenient. They are also safer (2) (using / to use) than cars.

(1) _____

(2) _____

27. 다음 문장에서 어법상 <u>어색한</u> 부분을 찾아 바르게 고쳐 쓰시오. (4점)

> Do you remember meet Jeff last summer?

→ _____

28. 두 문장이 같은 뜻이 되도록 빈칸에 알맞은 말을 쓰시오. (4점)

> Nadya likes to send text messages.

→ Nadya enjoys _____ text messages.

29. 우리말 의미에 맞도록 주어진 단어를 알맞게 배열하여 문장을 완성하시오. (5점)

> 너는 열 여섯살이 되기를 기대하고 있니?

→ Are you _____

_____ to 16?

(to / forward / looking / turning)

30. 다음 글을 읽고 주어진 단어를 활용하여 요약문을 완성하시오. (5점)

> Do you bite your nails? Many people have this bad habit, and they have trouble stopping it. But there are ways. One way is to cover your nails with bandages. Then you can't bite them. Also, people usually bite their nails because of stress. So it's important to relax. Exercise or a new hobby might help.

↓

> [**Summary**]
> It's not easy to quit (1) _____ (bite) your nails, but you can do it. Try (2) _____ (cover) them with bandages. And remember (3) _____ (relax).

(1) _____

(2) _____

(3) _____

11 분사

1 분사의 개념과 종류

1 분사의 개념: 분사는 〈동사원형 + -ing/-ed〉의 형태로 형용사의 역할을 한다. 또한 동사의 성질을 갖고 있어서 be 동사나 have 동사와 결합하여 서술어를 이루기도 한다.

Look at the **falling** leaves. ("떨어지고 있는")
Look at the **fallen** leaves on the ground. ("떨어진")

2 분사의 종류

1> 현재분사: 〈동사원형 + -ing〉의 형태로 일반적으로 능동/진행의 의미를 나타낸다.
Never wake a **sleeping** baby.
The **singing** parrot amazed everyone.
The cat is **sleeping** in the bowl.

2> 과거분사: 〈동사원형 + -ed〉의 형태로 일반적으로 수동/완료/상태의 의미를 나타낸다.
We can all see that the windows are **broken**.
I found my **lost** watch under my bed.
Thousands of children are **born** every day.
My sister is **married** to a lawyer.

Pop Quiz

✎ 괄호 안의 표현 중 알맞은 것을 고르시오.

1. My French class was really (boring / bored).
2. This store sells a lot of (freezing / frozen) food.
3. This map of the park is (confusing / confused).
4. The story had a (surprising / surprised) ending.
5. Do you drink (bottling / bottled) water?

 **분사의 쓰임새**

형용사 역할	명사 수식	명사의 앞이나 뒤에서 명사를 꾸며준다.
	주격보어 및 목적격보어	주어 및 목적어의 상태나 동작을 설명한다.
서술어 역할	be + 현재분사 (진행형)	어떤 동작이 진행 중임을 나타낸다.
	be + 과거분사 (수동태)	어떤 행위가 이루어졌음을 나타낸다.
	have + 과거분사 (완료형)	어떤 행위를 완료했음을 나타낸다.

❶ 분사가 단독으로 수식할 때는 명사 앞에서, 수식어구가 붙어 길어지면 명사 뒤에서 수식한다.
Falling leaves are beautiful.
Leaves **falling on the ground** are beautiful.

❷ 분사가 주어나 목적어의 상태를 설명할 때 현재분사는 능동, 과거분사는 수동의 의미를 갖는다.
New York City looks **amazing** from the top of the Empire State Building.
Do you hear the birds **singing**?
The boy was really **tired** from school.
Ed seemed **confused** to see Alex at Susie's birthday party.

❸ **Be** 동사 뒤에 현재분사가 오면 동작의 진행을 나타내는 진행형 시제가 된다.
Autumn leaves **are falling** on the ground.
Kelly **was playing** the guitar, and I **was singing**.

❹ **Be** 동사 뒤에 과거분사가 오면 수동태가 되어 문장의 주어는 행위의 주체가 아니라 행위의 대상이다.
Ketchup **is made** from tomatoes.
The Lord of the Rings **was written** by J. R. R. Tolkien.

❺ **Have** 동사 뒤에 과거분사를 쓰면 행위의 완료, 계속, 경험, 결과 등을 나타내는 완료형이 된다.
I **have fallen** in love with soccer.
Claire **has** already **spent** all her money.
I **have** never **eaten** snails.

 Pop Quiz

✎ 괄호 안의 표현 중 알맞은 것을 고르시오.

1. Maya is (leaving / left) for New Zealand soon.
2. A lot of flowers are (grew / grown) in the Netherlands.
3. That old house looks (frightening / frightened) at night.
4. Have you ever (seeing / seen) an elephant?
5. Didn't you hear your name (calling / called)?

3 분사와 To 부정사

현재분사 및 과거분사는 명사의 앞이나 뒤에서 명사를 수식할 수 있는데, **to** 부정사는 명사 뒤에서만 명사를 수식할 수 있다.

① 분사의 명사 수식

Did you have an **amazing dream** last night?
I found **something interesting** in this photo.
A **girl named Sue** called you this morning.

② **To** 부정사의 형용사적 용법

Playing computer games is my favorite **thing to do** on Sundays.
Would you like **something to drink**?
My brother has five **baby birds to take care of**.

4 분사와 동명사

현재분사와 동명사는 둘 다 〈동사원형 + -ing〉로 이루어지지만, 현재분사는 주로 형용사 역할을 하고 동명사는 명사 역할을 한다.

① 현재분사

Learning a foreign language is always **exciting**.
Water **falling** from the sky isn't **surprising**.

② 동명사

Swimming in the ocean at night is dangerous.
On weekends, I enjoy **swimming**, **inline skating**, or **riding a bike**.

Pop Quiz

A. 괄호 안의 표현 중 알맞은 것을 고르시오.

1. There is a quicker way (getting / to get) to Bill's house.

2. Be careful of the (broken / to break) glass.

3. We did nothing (exciting / to excite) over the weekend.

4. Do you need something (writing / to write) with?

B. 밑줄 친 단어가 현재분사인지 동명사인지 쓰시오.

1. The boy <u>standing</u> near the door is Jake.　　　　　(　　　　　　　)

2. <u>Wearing</u> glasses makes people look smart.　　　　(　　　　　　　)

3. Would you mind <u>giving</u> Sarah your seat?　　　　　(　　　　　　　)

4. Hurry and eat that <u>melting</u> ice cream.　　　　　　(　　　　　　　)

A. 주어진 단어를 알맞은 형태로 바꾸어 쓰시오.

1. The crowd was _____ loudly for their team. cheer
2. The _____ sun started to make the sky red. rise
3. I had never _____ Doug before yesterday. meet
4. Everyone felt _____ after the difficult lesson. confuse
5. We can't get in—the door is _____. lock

B. 괄호 안의 표현 중 알맞은 것을 고르시오.

1. This cough medicine tastes (disgusting / disgusted).
2. Nick has (missing / missed) three days of school.
3. My shirt is (making / made) of silk.
4. Chris hurt her leg (playing / played) basketball today.
5. All of your questions will be (answering / answered).

C. 다음 문장에서 어법상 <u>어색한</u> 부분을 찾아 바르게 고쳐 쓰시오.

1. All the tickets for the concert have been sell.

    → _____

2. We're always so boring on rainy Sunday afternoons.

    → _____

3. Bridget walked into the room smiled brightly.

    → _____

4. Cooking noodles are very soft.

    → _____

5. There are two people argue in the hallway.

    → _____

D. 우리말 의미에 맞도록 문장을 완성하시오.

1. Nancy has three _____.
   (낸시에게는 돌봐야 할 세 명의 자녀가 있다.)

2. We use a textbook _____.
   (우리는 우리 선생님이 쓴 교과서를 사용한다.)

3. _____ is exciting for young people.
   (운전을 배우는 것은 젊은 사람들에게 신나는 일이다.)

4. A bat looks like _____.
   (박쥐는 날아다니는 쥐처럼 생겼다.)

5. The kids _____ are completely wet.
   (빗속에서 놀고 있는 아이들은 완전히 젖었다.)

내신 대비 실전문제

이름: | 시간: 40분 | 점수: /100

선택형 (문항당 3점)

1. 다음 대화의 빈칸에 들어갈 말로 알맞은 것은?

> A: Why don't you play sports?
> B: I'm not _____ in them.

① interest
② interesting
③ interested
④ interests
⑤ be interested

2. 다음 문장의 밑줄 친 부분과 쓰임이 같은 것은?

> We're <u>listening</u> to music.

① It is <u>raining</u> hard.
② This is a <u>boring</u> subject.
③ The news was <u>surprising</u>.
④ Is the game <u>confusing</u>?
⑤ Greg told an <u>amazing</u> story.

3. 다음 중 밑줄 친 부분의 쓰임이 어색한 것은?

① The audience looks <u>bored</u>.
② Those walls are not <u>painted</u>.
③ We can skate on the <u>frozen</u> lake.
④ Rita gave me a <u>written</u> message.
⑤ I don't like <u>frightened</u> movies.

4. 다음 대화의 빈칸에 들어갈 말로 알맞지 <u>않은</u> 것은?

> A: What else do we need for the recipe?
> B: We need three _____ onions.

① large
② sliced
③ fresh
④ frying
⑤ boiled

5. 다음 중 밑줄 친 부분의 쓰임이 <u>다른</u> 하나는?

① Have you <u>seen</u> my watch?
② Violet has a <u>broken</u> leg.
③ I've <u>been</u> to Spain twice.
④ They haven't <u>missed</u> a class.
⑤ We have <u>chosen</u> a new president.

6. 다음 대화의 빈칸에 들어갈 말로 알맞은 것은?

> A: Is that amusement park fun?
> B: Yes, it has some _____ rides.

① exciting
② excited
③ excites
④ excite
⑤ to excite

7. 다음 빈칸에 들어갈 말로 알맞게 짝지은 것은?

> • The house was _____ ten years ago.
> • Nora was _____ on her cell phone.

① building – talked
② build – talk
③ built – talked
④ built – talking
⑤ building – talking

8. 빈칸에 들어갈 말로 알맞은 것은?

> This morning, my family and I went hiking on a mountain near our home. It took us three hours to reach the top. We were _____, but the view was beautiful!

① tire
② tiring
③ tired
④ tires
⑤ be tired

9. 다음 중 밑줄 친 부분의 쓰임이 같은 것끼리 묶인 것은?

> a. <u>Playing</u> volleyball is pretty easy.
> b. The guy <u>playing</u> the drums was Ken.
> c. Do you spend much time <u>playing</u> games?
> d. I like to watch the puppies <u>playing</u>.
> e. I remember <u>playing</u> soccer as a kid.

① (a, c, e) – (b, d)
② (a, e) – (b, c, d)
③ (a, d) – (b, c, e)
④ (a, c) – (b, d, e)
⑤ (a, b, e) – (c, d)

10. 다음 빈칸에 들어갈 말로 알맞게 짝지은 것은?

> • Do you hear someone _____?
> • That song hasn't been _____ yet.

① sing – singing
② singing – sung
③ singing – singing
④ sung – sang
⑤ sang – sung

11. 다음 중 밑줄 친 부분의 쓰임이 <u>다른</u> 하나는?

① <u>Eating</u> lunch doesn't take long.
② We enjoy <u>eating</u> lunch together.
③ They look forward to <u>eating</u> lunch.
④ Jeff and I were <u>eating</u> lunch earlier.
⑤ Myra loves <u>eating</u> lunch outside.

12. 다음 빈칸에 공통으로 들어갈 말로 알맞은 것은?

> • _____ fruit is a delicious snack.
> • I had _____ the dishes before I put them away.

① dry   ② to dry
③ dries   ④ dried
⑤ drying

13. 다음 중 밑줄 친 부분의 쓰임이 <u>다른</u> 하나는?

① The girl <u>sitting</u> next to me was Kelly.
② I saw you <u>sitting</u> in the teacher's chair.
③ Who was the person <u>sitting</u> by the door?
④ No one <u>sitting</u> at the back can hear the speaker.
⑤ My back hurts from <u>sitting</u> all day long.

14. 다음 문장의 밑줄 친 부분과 쓰임이 같은 것은?

> Mario wants to take <u>singing</u> lessons.

① The sun is <u>shining</u> brightly.
② My cat hates <u>taking</u> baths.
③ Gail was <u>waiting</u> for you.
④ Use <u>boiling</u> water to make tea.
⑤ Deirdre has a <u>talking</u> bird.

15. 다음 중 밑줄 친 부분의 쓰임이 옳은 것은?

① The class felt <u>worrying</u> about the quiz.
② A woman <u>getting</u> on the bus almost fell.
③ I'm <u>confusing</u> about the meaning of this word.
④ All the tickets have been <u>selling</u> already.
⑤ Stores were <u>closing</u> for two days because of Chuseok.

16. 다음 중 밑줄 친 부분의 쓰임이 같은 것끼리 묶인 것은?

> a. Who <u>made</u> this mess?
> b. Jean gladly <u>made</u> the birthday cake.
> c. I like soup <u>made</u> with garlic.
> d. Were your clothes <u>made</u> in China?
> e. These toys are <u>made</u> of plastic.

① (a, c) – (b, d, e)
② (a, c, e) – (b, d)
③ (a, b, d) – (c, e)
④ (a, d) – (b, c, e)
⑤ (a, b) – (c, d, e)

17. 다음 중 밑줄 친 부분의 쓰임이 옳은 것은?

① Would you like something <u>drink</u>?

② His favorite exercise is <u>ride</u> a bike.

③ Mark told us something <u>exciting</u>.

④ Everyone was <u>to laughing</u> at the joke.

⑤ I wore a <u>frightened</u> mask on Halloween.

18. 다음 빈칸에 들어갈 말로 알맞게 짝지은 것은?

> • Is there anything _____ on TV tonight?
> • A girl _____ down the street waved at me.

① to watch – walking

② watched – walking

③ to watch – walked

④ watching – to walk

⑤ watched – to walk

19. 다음 대화의 밑줄 친 부분 중 어법상 옳은 것은?

> A: What's that great smell ① <u>to come</u> from the kitchen?
> B: I am ② <u>bake</u> some cookies.
> A: Great! I love freshly ③ <u>baked</u> cookies.
> B: Why don't you learn ④ <u>making</u> them yourself?
> A: It's no use ⑤ <u>to try</u>. I'm terrible at cooking.

①   ②   ③   ④   ⑤

20. 다음 대화의 빈칸에 들어갈 말로 알맞은 것은?

> A: I get so many spam text messages. I hate them!
> B: Me, too. They're really _____.

① annoying   ② annoyed

③ annoys   ④ to annoy

⑤ annoy

21. 우리말 의미에 맞도록 문장을 완성하시오. (3점)

> 우리는 오늘 밤에 끝내야 할 숙제가 세 개 있다.

→ We have three assignments _____ tonight.

22. 다음 밑줄 친 부분을 바르게 고쳐 쓰시오. (3점)

> Dad needs someone <u>help</u> him fix the car.

→ _____

23. 다음 중 밑줄 친 부분의 쓰임이 <u>어색한</u> 것을 골라 바르게 고쳐 쓰시오. (4점)

> ① Ben hasn't <u>quit</u> his part-time job yet.
> ② Italy is a country <u>known</u> for good food.
> ③ Give your <u>finished</u> project to the teacher.
> ④ It was <u>amazed</u> to meet my favorite actress.
> ⑤ Was Charlie <u>disappointed</u> to miss the party?

→ _____

24. 두 문장이 같은 뜻이 되도록 빈칸에 알맞은 단어를 쓰시오. (4점)

> I love the band. It is playing now.

→ I love the band _____ now.

25. 다음 문장에서 어법상 <u>어색한</u> 부분을 찾아 바르게 고쳐 쓰시오. (4점)

> Who is that handsome man talk to Dylan?

→ _____

26. 우리말 의미에 맞도록 문장을 완성하시오. (4점)

이곳 학생들이 입고 있는 교복은 짙은 녹색이다.

→ The uniforms _____
   by students here are dark green.

27. 다음 문장에서 어법상 <u>어색한</u> 부분을 찾아 바르게 고쳐 쓰시오. (4점)

Did Nathan find his losing wallet?

→ _____

28. 괄호 안의 단어 중 알맞은 것을 골라 순서대로 쓰시오. (4점)

I like my bedroom. It is (1) (decorating / decorated) with my favorite things. A big picture (2) (hangs / hanging) above my bed shows my favorite soccer team, Manchester United.

(1) _____

(2) _____

29. 우리말 의미에 맞도록 주어진 단어를 알맞게 배열하시오. (5점)

미소 짓는 소녀는 치킨을 먹고 있다.

→ _____

(girl / fried / the / smiling / chicken / eating / is)

30. 다음 글을 읽고 밑줄 친 우리말을 영어로 옮겨 쓰시오. (5점)

Book Review:
Charlie and the Chocolate Factory

This is a wonderful story about Charlie, a boy from a poor family. One day, he and four other kids win a trip to a candy factory. Of course, (1) <u>찰리는 아주 신이 난다</u>. At the factory, (2) <u>많은 놀라운 일들이 벌어진다</u>. (3) <u>이 책은 전혀 지루하지 않다</u>. It is funny and has a happy ending. Everyone should read it!

(1) _____

(2) _____

(3) _____

접속사와 전치사

Chapter 12 접속사와 전치사

1 등위접속사

대등한 문장 요소(명사, 동사, 형용사, 부사, 구, 절)를 연결하는 역할을 하며 **and, but, or, yet, for, so, nor**가 있다.

✔ **구와 절**: 두 개 이상이 단어가 결합하여 의미를 형성하는 문장 요소를 구(phrase)라고 하며, 두 개 이상의 단어가 〈주어 + 동사〉의 형태를 이루는 경우에 절(clause)이라고 한다.

1 단어나 구를 연결하는 등위접속사

1> 역할

Jane **and** Mary are best friends. (명사 연결)
Every morning they cook breakfast **and** wash the dishes. (동사 연결)
They are poor **but** hard-working students. (형용사 연결)
They want to live in the country **or** in a small town. (부사구 연결)

2> 의미

Jane is intelligent **and** polite. (추가)
Jane is intelligent **but** impolite. (대조)
I don't think Jane is intelligent **or** polite. (선택)

2 절을 연결하는 등위접속사

- 절을 연결하는 등위접속사 앞에 쉼표(,)를 쓰는 것이 원칙이지만 연결된 두 절 모두 짧은 경우에는 쉼표를 생략하기도 한다.

Jane is cute **and** her sister is beautiful. (추가)
Jane is beautiful, **but** her sister is not very good-looking. (대조)
Jim fell asleep during the movie. The movie was boring, **or** he was very tired. (둘 중 하나)
Jane was delighted, **for** her essay won the grand prize on the contest. (이유)

Pop Quiz

 괄호 안의 표현 중 알맞은 것을 고르시오.

1. Let's cut some vegetables (and / or) put them in a bowl.

2. Which do you like better, hamburgers (but / or) pizza?

3. I'm often late, (and / but) I arrived right on time today.

4. Joan was worried, (but / for) her son was traveling alone.

5. Summer is almost over, (so / or) the weather is getting cool.

6. It started to rain, (but / so) I took an umbrella.

7. I know how to play the drums (and / or) the guitar.

8. My sister likes ketchup, (or / yet) she hates tomatoes.

2 종속접속사

주절의 의미를 보충하는 절을 종속절이라고 한다. 이때 사용되는 **as, because, since, though, when, if, before, after** 등의 접속사를 종속접속사라고 하고 이러한 접속사로 시작하는 절을 종속절(부사절)이라고 한다.

Mary was disappointed **because** her grades were not good enough. (이유)
As they were in a hurry, they didn't eat dessert. (이유)
Mary was going home **when** she got a phone call from her mother. (시간)
You stay here **while** I talk to your teacher. (시간)
Dan has felt depressed **since** Gene left him. (since 다음에 과거의 사건이 나오면 주절은 현재완료가 된다.)
Though/Although she worked hard, Mary's grades were not very good. (양보)
If it rains tomorrow, the game will be canceled. (조건)

3 접속부사

주로 문장 맨 앞에서 바로 앞에 있는 문장과의 논리적 관계를 전달하는 부사를 접속부사라 하며, 바로 뒤에 쉼표를 쓴다. 문장 중간이나 끝에 오는 경우도 있다.

① 대조 : however, nevertheless, nonetheless, still 등
Herman grew up in Colorado. **However**, Doug came from Utah.

② 결과 : accordingly, consequently, hence, therefore, thus 등
He was very sick. **Therefore**, he didn't go to school.

③ 부가 설명 : further, in addition, furthermore, moreover 등
Dan did not discuss the matter with Jill. **Furthermore**, he didn't even contact her.

④ 기타 : meanwhile, instead, of course, otherwise 등

Pop Quiz

A. 부사절에 밑줄을 긋고 용법(시간, 이유, 조건, 양보)을 쓰시오.

1. Sally fell off the ladder when she was painting the ceiling. (   )
2. People like Eric because he is very friendly. (   )
3. You can have a sandwich if you want. (   )
4. Since Joseph is bad at card games, he doesn't like them. (   )
5. Although the weather was not good, we had a great time. (   )

B. 괄호 안의 표현 중 알맞은 것을 고르시오.

1. Your computer won't arrive till Monday. (Meanwhile / Moreover), you can use Jim's.
2. No one complained about the mess; (accordingly / however), they didn't clean it up.
3. Becoming a doctor is not easy. (Consequently / Nonetheless), I know you can do it.
4. Large diamonds are not very common; (further / thus), they are expensive.
5. The movie had exciting action. (Furthermore / Still), the acting was great.

A. 빈칸에 알맞은 등위접속사를 골라 문장을 완성하시오.

and	but	or	for	so

1. Philip's tooth hurt, _____ he went to the dentist.
2. Would you like to eat at home _____ eat out?
3. Please stop at the store _____ get some shampoo.
4. The people hoped for peace, _____ they hated war.
5. My new jeans are cheap _____ well-made.

B. 빈칸에 알맞은 종속접속사를 골라 문장을 완성하시오.

when	though	if	before	because

1. _____ you're cold, put on a sweater.
2. I always have fun _____ I'm with you.
3. Students must raise their hands _____ they speak.
4. _____ my aunt reads a lot, she has a big vocabulary.
5. _____ Kyle ate a huge breakfast, he's very hungry.

C. 빈칸에 알맞은 접속부사를 골라 문장을 완성하시오.

however	thus	moreover	therefore	nonetheless

1. It hasn't rained for a long time. _____, the grass is turning brown.
2. Emma was telling the truth; _____, no one believed her.
3. The joke wasn't funny at all; _____, it was unkind.
4. Mr. Tanaka is 85 years old. _____, he is healthier than many young men.
5. I'm a vegetarian; _____, I don't eat fish.

D. 우리말 의미에 맞도록 문장을 완성하시오.

1. You should return the book _____.
   (도서관이 문을 닫기 전에 그 책을 반납해야 합니다.)

2. Marian's parents bought her a kitten _____.
   (마리앤의 부모님은 마리앤이 강아지를 원했지만 고양이를 사주었다.)

3. Don likes to listen to his MP3 player _____.
   (돈은 지하철을 타고 있는 동안 MP3 플레이어를 듣는 것을 좋아한다.)

4. I won't get enough sleep tonight _____.
   (내가 새벽 2시에 잠을 자면 오늘밤에 잠을 충분히 자지 못하게 된다.)

5. Nurses have interesting jobs. _____.
   (간호사는 흥미로운 일이 많다. 게다가 그들은 많은 사람을 도와준다.)

4 전치사

① 장소의 전치사

at	~에서	Terry met his mom **at** the mall.
in	~안에	Fruit has lots of sugar **in** it.
on	~위에	What is that red spot **on** your face?
by	~곁에	Morley gently put the little dog **by** the door.
under	~아래	There's nothing new **under** the sun.

② 시간의 전치사

in + 년/월/계절/세기	**in** 2011, **in** December, **in** the winter, **in** the 18th century
at + 시각/시점	**at** 7 o'clock, **at** night, **at** dawn, **at** midnight, **at** noon
on + 날짜/요일	**on** March 10, **on** Sunday, **on** Saturday morning
for + 불특정 기간	Hold your breath **for** a few seconds and drink water.
during + 특정 기간	**During** her visit to the zoo, something terrible happened.
before/after + 특정 시점	They talked over the project **before** class.

③ 기타 전치사

Roy didn't study **for** the test. ("~을 위하여")
It was a very difficult decision **for** Mike. ("~로서는")
I want to talk **about** the trip next month. ("~에 관하여")
Francine asked Andy to have lunch **with** her. ("~와 함께")
Darren helps them **with** their homework. ("~에 관하여": 도와주는 일)
Look at that woman **in** the fur coat. ("~을 입고": 복장)
Gerald watched a great movie **on** TV last night. ("~에": 특정 기기)

Pop Quiz

A. 빈칸에 알맞은 전치사를 쓰시오.

1. We get up early _____ Monday mornings.
2. The boat was sailing _____ the bridge.
3. Eating makes Grandma sleepy, so she takes a nap _____ lunch.
4. Never use your cell phone _____ the flight.

B. 괄호 안의 표현 중 알맞은 것을 고르시오.

1. I heard the news (on / with) the radio.
2. Jim saw a woman dressed (in / on) silk at the party.
3. Liz helped Paul (about / with) some difficult math questions.
4. Running ten kilometers seems easy (for / on) you.

5 전치사의 관용적 표현

❶ 형용사 뒤에 오는 전치사

1> be + sure/afraid/ignorant/full/free/aware/reminded/ashamed + of + 명사
Polly was sure **of** her success.

2> be + similar/equal/essential/indifferent/married/devoted/opposed + to + 명사
The money is essential **to** his success.

3> be + responsible/thankful/necessary/blamed/praised/mistaken + for + 명사
His smartness was responsible **for** Jim's success.

4> be + different/absent/safe + from + 명사
Danny was absent **from** school yesterday.

5> be + surprised/amazed + at + 명사
Bob was amazed **at** the peace and quiet at the park.

6> be + satisfied/covered/filled/bored/confused + with + 명사
The bag is filled **with** mysterious letters.

7> be + interested/dressed/lost + in + 명사
Dan's mother was dressed **in** luxurious silk.

❷ 동사 뒤에 오는 전치사

Did Craig **drop by** your house?
Joan **looked for** a new car.
Tom **listens to** jazz every day.

- 동사가 전치사적 부사와 결합하기도 하는데, 목적어는 둘 사이에 끼어들어 〈동사 + 목적어 + 전치사적 부사〉 형태가 되기도 한다. 이때 목적어가 대명사이면 〈동사 + 목적어 + 전치사적 부사〉의 어순이 된다.
My dad **grew up** in the country.
Barney **figured out** the answer. (→ figured the answer **out** → figured it **out**)
Take off that horrible dress, honey! (→ take it **off**는 가능, **take** off **it**은 불가)

Pop Quiz

A. 괄호 안의 단어 중 알맞은 것을 고르시오.

1. The director was fully aware (of / with) the danger.

2. The student was thankful (at / for) Ms. McKinley's kindness.

3. Dugan's father is really devoted (for / to) his family.

4. Albert was satisfied (on / with) his assistant's work.

5. Aaron's mom was quite interested (at / in) celebrities.

B. 괄호 안의 표현 중 알맞은 것을 고르시오.

1. Can you pick (it up / up it) for me please?

2. Do you want me to turn (it off / off it), Dylan?

3. Larry failed to get (down / off) the bus.

4. Could you drop (by / off) at my office sometime?

5. The couple was looking (to / for) an affordable apartment.

A. 빈칸에 알맞은 시간 전치사를 골라 문장을 완성하시오.

during	for	before	in	after

1. We waited _____ fifteen minutes before we got a table.
2. Some animals are awake and active _____ the night.
3. _____ his workout, Matt took a shower and changed his clothes.
4. Korea usually has beautiful weather _____ May.
5. Our team had an extra practice _____ the final game.

B. 빈칸에 알맞은 장소 전치사를 골라 문장을 완성하시오.

at	by	under	on	about

1. I finally found my book on the floor _____ the sofa.
2. It was cold, so everyone wanted to sit _____ the fire.
3. This article is _____ the life of Abraham Lincoln.
4. Jude hopes to work _____ a bank after she graduates.
5. Dad has a picture of the whole family _____ his desk.

C. 빈칸에 알맞은 전치사를 골라 문장을 완성하시오.

of	to	for	from	with

1. High school seems very different _____ middle school.
2. The top of the mountain is always covered _____ snow.
3. Unfortunately, the wrong person was blamed _____ the mistake.
4. Many people are afraid _____ snakes and spiders.
5. That actor has been married _____ four different women.

D. 우리말 의미에 맞도록 문장을 완성하시오.

1. Miranda isn't _____ her new haircut.
   (미란다는 새로 자른 머리가 만족스럽지 않다.)

2. We _____ the teacher as she explained the test.
   (우리는 선생님이 시험에 관해 설명할 때 귀 기울여 들었다.)

3. Since I didn't know that word, I had to _____ in the dictionary.
   (나는 그 단어를 몰랐기 때문에 그것을 사전에서 찾아보아야 했다.)

4. Doctors are strongly _____ smoking.
   (의사들은 흡연에 강력히 반대한다.)

5. Mickey felt _____ his rudeness, and he apologized.
   (미키는 자신의 무례가 부끄러워서 사과했다.)

내신 대비 실전문제

이름: | 시간: 40분 | 점수: /100

선택형 (문항당 3점)

1. 다음 대화의 빈칸에 들어갈 말로 알맞은 것은?

> A: What kinds of music do you like, Renee?
> B: My favorites are rock _____ pop.

① or   ② and
③ so   ④ for
⑤ but

2. 다음 중 접속사 but이 들어가기에 알맞은 위치는?

> Our trip ① to ② the country ③ yesterday
> ④ was tiring ⑤ really fun.

①   ②   ③   ④   ⑤

3. 다음 중 빈칸에 접속사 so가 들어가기에 어색한 것은?
① Minnie wants to learn to surf, _____ Craig is teaching her.
② Forests help clean the air, _____ they are very important.
③ Hana has never been abroad, _____ she speaks three languages.
④ I showered and took a short nap, _____ I feel much better.
⑤ The noise was very loud, _____ it scared the baby.

4. 빈칸에 들어갈 말로 알맞은 것은?

> Ginny read a magazine _____ she waited to see the doctor.

① so   ② since
③ though   ④ while
⑤ because

5. 다음 빈칸에 공통으로 들어갈 말로 알맞은 것은?

> • _____ Ken had a part-time job, he always needed money.
> • _____ we hiked to the top of the mountain, we weren't tired.

① Though   ② Because
③ Since   ④ If
⑤ As

6. 다음 빈칸에 들어갈 말로 알맞게 짝지은 것은?

> • _____ we have a quiz today, I'm going to fail it.
> • Rita arrived late _____ she missed her bus.

① As – although
② Although – as
③ If – while
④ If – as
⑤ As – although

7. 다음 문장의 밑줄 친 부분과 쓰임이 다른 하나는?

> Edward has come back to visit twice <u>since</u> he and his family moved away.

① We can't play chess <u>since</u> several pieces are missing.
② No one is going swimming <u>since</u> the water's so cold.
③ Your little brother has grown a lot <u>since</u> I last saw him.
④ Today's class was canceled <u>since</u> only two students came.
⑤ They want seafood <u>since</u> they haven't had any for a while.

8. 빈칸에 들어갈 말로 알맞지 <u>않은</u> 것은?

> _____ pets aren't allowed in this apartment building, we can't get a cat.

① If   ② Since
③ As   ④ Because
⑤ Though

9. 다음 빈칸에 공통으로 들어갈 말로 알맞은 것은?

> • Rachael will graduate from high school _____ the spring of 2015.
> • Is there a lot of meat _____ this soup?

① on   ② at
③ in   ④ by
⑤ of

10. 빈칸에 들어갈 말로 알맞은 것은?

> Busan is Korea's second-largest city and one of the world's busiest ports. _____, the world's biggest department store, Shinsegae Centum City, is located there.

① Furthermore   ② Therefore
③ Because   ④ Still
⑤ However

11. 빈칸에 들어갈 말로 알맞지 <u>않은</u> 것은?

> Next Wednesday, December 17th, is a holiday (Election Day). _____, this office will be closed.

① Accordingly   ② Consequently
③ Therefore   ④ Thus
⑤ Because

12. 다음 대화의 빈칸에 들어갈 말로 알맞은 것은?

> A: Our science project isn't due until the end of the month, so there's no need to hurry.
> B: I know. _____, we should get started on our research soon.

① Still   ② Furthermore
③ And   ④ Moreover
⑤ So

13. 다음 빈칸에 공통으로 들어갈 말로 알맞은 것은?

> • Stella gets a lot of her designer clothes _____ that store.
> • It's traditional to kiss someone _____ midnight on New Year's Eve.

① at   ② in
③ on   ④ by
⑤ from

14. 다음 중 밑줄 친 전치사의 쓰임이 <u>다른</u> 하나는?

① Molly plans to study abroad <u>for</u> one semester.
② Do you mind if we sit and rest <u>for</u> a while?
③ Lisa has been taking dance lessons <u>for</u> nearly a year.
④ How long will we have to wait <u>for</u> the test results?
⑤ Dan can hold his breath <u>for</u> over three minutes.

15. 다음 빈칸에 들어갈 말로 알맞게 짝지은 것은?

> • Kelly's new hairstyle is quite similar _____ yours.
> • We were all amazed _____ Mike's magic tricks.

① with – by
② to – at
③ of – by
④ with – at
⑤ to – from

16. 우리말 의미에 맞도록 할 때 빈칸에 알맞은 말은?

> 나는 식사 도중에 전화를 받는 것은 예의에 어긋난다고 생각해.
>
> = I think it's rude to answer your phone _____ a meal.

① after   ② as
③ for   ④ during
⑤ while

17. 다음 중 밑줄 친 부분을 옳게 고쳐 쓴 것은?

> If you are looking <u>to</u> the soda, it is in aisle 8.

① by   ② of
③ for   ④ on
⑤ at

18. 다음 빈칸에 들어갈 말로 알맞게 짝지은 것은?

> • My sister has always dreamed _____ becoming a pilot.
> • Dave is watching an old movie _____ channel 5.

① of – at
② about – on
③ of – in
④ for – in
⑤ for – on

19. 우리말 의미에 맞도록 할 때 빈칸에 알맞은 말은?

> 릴리는 바이올린 연주회에 대비하여 열심히 연습해 왔다.
>
> = Lily has been practicing hard to prepare _____ her violin recital.

① to   ② with
③ by   ④ on
⑤ for

20. 다음 빈칸에 공통으로 들어갈 말로 알맞은 것은?

> • Would you please help me _____ the housework?
> • Annette didn't want to walk home alone, so Craig went _____ her.

① to   ② for
③ with   ④ from
⑤ about

서술형

21. 다음 빈칸에 들어갈 알맞은 접속부사를 쓰시오. (3점)

> Everyone knows that it's important to exercise at least three times a week; _____, many people fail to do so.

→ _____

22. 다음 빈칸에 들어갈 말을 순서대로 쓰시오. (3점)

> • This lotion will keep you safe (1) _____ sunburn.
> • Which school subjects is Tom most interested (2) _____?

(1) _____

(2) _____

23. 다음 빈칸에 공통으로 들어갈 전치사를 쓰시오. (4점)

> • The firefighter was praised _____ saving the child.
> • Parents are responsible _____ their children's education.

→ _____

24. 다음 중 밑줄 친 부분의 쓰임이 어색한 것을 골라 바르게 고쳐 쓰시오. (4점)

> ① Please don't forget to take up the garbage.
> ② Ali usually wakes up when the sun rises.
> ③ I'll hang up your coat in the hall closet.
> ④ What do you need to look up in the encyclopedia?
> ⑤ They were born in the US but grew up in Korea.

→ _____

25. 두 문장이 같은 뜻이 되도록 빈칸에 알맞은 접속사를 쓰시오. (4점)

> Although these jeans are old and have a hole in them, I love them.

→ These jeans are old and have a hole in them, _____ I love them.

26. 다음 빈칸에 들어갈 말을 순서대로 쓰시오. (4점)

> (1) The paint on this bench is still wet, _____ don't touch it.
> (2) Steve poured a tall glass of water _____ drank it all.

(1) _____

(2) _____

27. 다음 밑줄 친 단어와 바꾸어 쓸 수 있는 전치사를 쓰시오. (4점)

> Who is that woman wearing the red scarf?

→ _____

28. 우리말 의미에 맞도록 문장을 완성하시오. (4점)

> 이 영화를 내려받는 데는 약 15분이 걸릴 거야. 그동안 우리는 다른 것을 볼 수 있어.

→ The movie will finish downloading in about fifteen minutes. _____, we can watch something else.

고난도 서술형

29. 우리말 의미에 맞도록 주어진 단어를 알맞게 배열하시오. (5점)

> 카렌은 신발이 불편해서 벗어버렸다.

→ _____

_____

(uncomfortable / Karen's shoes / took / were / off / so / them / she)

30. 다음 글을 읽고 빈칸에 알맞은 접속부사를 순서대로 쓰시오. (5점)

> Asian elephants are beautiful animals. They used to live all over Asia. (1) _____, now they live only in the south and southeast of Asia. One reason is that people destroyed their homes by farming and cutting down trees. (2) _____, many have been killed by hunters. (3) _____, now there are only about 40,000 Asian elephants in the world.

(1) _____

(2) _____

(3) _____

Appendix

✎ 불규칙 동사 변화표

1> ABB형

원형	과거형	과거분사형
bring	brought	brought
build	built	built
buy	bought	bought
catch	caught	caught
feed	fed	fed
feel	felt	felt
fight	fought	fought
find	found	found
have	had	had
hear	heard	heard
hold	held	held
keep	kept	kept
leave	left	left
lend	lent	lent
lose	lost	lost
make	made	made
meet	met	met
pay	paid	paid
say	said	said
sell	sold	sold
send	sent	sent
sleep	slept	slept
spend	spent	spent
stand	stood	stood
teach	taught	taught
think	thought	thought
understand	understood	understood
win	won	won

2> ABA형

원형	과거형	과거분사형
become	became	become
come	came	come
run	ran	run

3> AAA형

원형	과거형	과거분사형
cost	cost	cost
cut	cut	cut
hit	hit	hit
hurt	hurt	hurt
let	let	let
put	put	put
read	read	read
set	set	set

4> ABC형

원형	과거형	과거분사형
bear	bore	born
begin	began	begun
bite	bit	bitten
break	broke	broken
choose	chose	chosen
do	did	done
draw	drew	drawn
drive	drove	driven
eat	ate	eaten
fall	fell	fallen
get	got	got / gotten
give	gave	given
go	went	gone
grow	grew	grown
mistake	mistook	mistaken
ride	rode	ridden
ring	rang	rung
rise	rose	risen
see	saw	seen
sing	sang	sung
speak	spoke	spoken
swim	swam	swum
take	took	taken
throw	threw	thrown
wear	wore	worn
write	wrote	written

『Quattro』 시리즈

Quattro Grammar Start, Jump, Master

Quattro Listening Start, Jump, Master

Quattro Reading Start A-C, Jump A-C, Master A-C

Quattro Series Level Chart

	Titles	중등 1			중등 2			중등 3		
NEW	Quattro Grammar	Start			Jump			Master		
NEW	Quattro Listening	Start			Jump			Master		
	Quattro Reading Start A-C	Start A	Start B	Start C						
	Quattro Reading Jump A-C				Jump A	Jump B	Jump C			
	Quattro Reading Master A-C							Master A	Master B	Master C

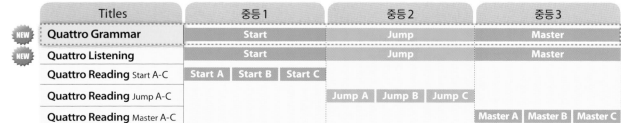

콰트로

Quattro Grammar

Start

정답 및 해설

Quattro Grammar

Start

NOUNS
ADVERB
SENTENCES
VERBS
ADJECTIVES

정답 및 해설

Chapter 1
문장의 종류와 문장 5형식

❶ 문장이란 무엇인가?

Pop Quiz → p. 12

A

1. X
2. O
3. O
4. X
5. O
6. X
7. X

B

3. Today is your lucky day.

❷ 문장의 종류

Pop Quiz → p. 13

A

1. don't / do not
2. didn't / did not
3. not

B

1. doesn't drink / does not drink
2. Don't talk / Do not talk
3. Let's stop

Pop Quiz → p. 14

A

1. Is
2. What
3. Does / Why does

B

1. wasn't it
2. do they
3. is he

Grammar Practice → p. 15

A

1. doesn't drive
2. don't speak
3. Don't hurry
4. didn't arrive
5. Don't the boys play

B

1. Do most children like
2. Did John and Amy go shopping
3. Was it raining
4. did she get up
5. didn't you show up

C

1. didn't we
2. don't you
3. doesn't he
4. did I
5. weren't they

D

1. are
2. doesn't end
3. don't like
4. What cute
5. does the concert start

❸ 문장의 주요 성분

Pop Quiz → p. 16

A

1. Sarah
2. Winning the race
3. you
4. Tina
5. My sister

B

1. the toys
2. a lot of food
3. walking
4. the book
5. Sandra

❹ 동사의 종류와 문장 5형식

Pop Quiz → p. 17

A

1. turned, (2)
2. fall, (1)
3. were, (2)

B

1. honest
2. terrible
3. angry

Pop Quiz → p. 18

1. made, (5)
2. want, (3)
3. gave, (4)
4. asked, (5)
5. grow, (3)

Grammar Practice → p. 19

A

1. My mom
2. a prince
3. English
4. a dog and three cats
5. Your dreams

B

1. felt, (2)
2. baked, (4)
3. turn, (2)
4. joined, (3)
5. happen, (1)

C

1. with long hair runs fast
2. was late for school yesterday
3. teaches the Little Prince great lessons
4. up the paper on the floor
5. drive me crazy

D

1. are playing tennis
2. finds her attractive
3. teaches children an important lesson
4. wrote a song for his girlfriend
5. sent me a long email yesterday

내신 대비 실전문제 → pp. 20-23

선택형

1. ②	2. ①	3. ③	4. ④	5. ④
6. ③	7. ①	8. ④	9. ②	10. ①
11. ②	12. ②	13. ①	14. ⑤	15. ①
16. ⑤	17. ⑤	18. ②	19. ③	20. ①

서술형

21. don't
22. wasn't it
23. ②, Our math teacher always makes us laugh.
24. play basketball or ride a bike / ride a bike or play basketball
25. The boy's cough didn't sound terrible.
26. a pretty doll you have
27. not start a fight
28. Don't let him pay for dinner.

고난도 서술형

29. didn't allow me to go
30. (1) You sent a wonderful gift to me.
    → You sent me a wonderful gift.
    (2) Mom and Dad bought me dinner at my favorite restaurant.
    → Mom and Dad bought dinner for me at my favorite restaurant.

[문제풀이]

선택형

1. 하나의 문장은 마침표나 물음표나 느낌표로 끝난다. ②는 접속사 When이 이끄는 부사절이며 문장 부호도 없으므로 문장이 아니다. ①은 의문문, ③은 감탄문, ④와 ⑤는 평서문이다.
2. 일반동사의 부정문은 <don't/doesn't + 동사원형>의 형태를 취하므로 동사원형 like가 맞다.
3. 일반동사가 있는 문장의 의문문은 <do/does/did + 주어 + 동사원형>의 순서이므로 ③의 went를 go로 바꿔야 한다.
4. 감탄문에서는 주어와 동사를 도치하지 않는다
   ④ → How lovely your eyes are!
5. 너(you)에게 물은 질문이므로 나(I)로 대답해야 하고, be 동사로 묻는 말에는 be 동사로 대답해야 하며, Yes 뒤에는 긍정, No 뒤에는 부정형을 써야 하므로 ④가 맞다.
6. 의문사로 묻는 의문문에 대한 대답에는 Yes/No를 사용하지 않는다.
7. 긍정문 You take ~에 대한 부가의문문은 부정의문문 형태인 don't you가 맞다.
8. 일반동사의 과거형 fell의 부정형은 <didn't + 동사원형>의 형태인 ④가 맞다.
9. ② → Do the girls wake up early on Sundays?
10. 명령문은 동사원형으로 시작하는데, ①에는 동사원형이 없다.
    ① → Please be careful when you drive.
11. 부가의문문에 대한 대답은 내용이 긍정이면 Yes, 부정이면 No로 대답한다.
12. ②의 주어는 복수인 flowers이므로 be 동사는 are가 맞다.
13. 지각동사 heard의 목적격보어로 동사원형 call이 맞다.
14. 2형식 동사 seem은 형용사 보어가 필요하며, 동생을 돌보느라 피곤한 상태를 나타내므로 tired가 맞다.

15. 지각동사와 사역동사의 목적격보어는 동사원형이므로 fix와 take가 맞다.
16. 감각을 나타내는 동사의 보어는 형용사 형태이므로 ⑤의 badly를 bad로 바꿔야 한다.
17. tell의 목적격보어로는 to 부정사가 오므로 ⑤의 sing을 to sing으로 고쳐야 알맞다.
18. be 동사나 상태의 변화를 나타내는 동사들 다음에는 형용사 보어가 온다. happen은 완전자동사로 보어를 필요로 하지 않는다.
19. ①, ②, ④, ⑤의 주어는 단수이므로 동사 역시 starts, leaves, enjoys, is로 고쳐야 한다.
20. 목적격보어가 될 수 있는 것은 명사와 형용사이므로 답은 ①이다.

서술형

21. 일반동사 learn, want, like를 부정하는 문장이므로 doesn't/don't가 답이 될 수 있는데, 주어가 복수이거나 2인칭이므로 don't를 써야 한다.
22. 문장의 주어가 3인칭 단수이고 동사가 was이므로 부가의문문은 wasn't it을 써야 한다.
23. 사역동사 make 뒤에는 〈목적어 + 동사원형〉이 온다.
24. 보기에 or가 있는 것으로 보아 선택의문문을 완성하는 문제임을 알 수 있다. 대답이 I ride a bike이므로 질문은 Do you play basketball or ride a bike?(또는 Do you ride a bike or play basketball?)가 맞다. 운동경기 앞에는 관사를 쓰지 않는 것에 유의한다.
25. 동사가 과거형인 sounded이므로 부정형은 didn't sound를 쓴다.
26. 감탄문의 어순은 〈What + 관사 + 형용사 + 명사 + 주어 + 동사!〉이다.
27. Let's의 부정형인 Let's not을 이용하여 문장을 완성한다.
28. 사역동사 let 뒤에는 〈목적어 + 동사원형〉이 온다.

고난도 서술형

29. allow의 과거 부정형인 didn't allow 뒤에 〈목적어 + to 부정사〉를 쓴다.
30. 4형식 문장을 3형식 문장으로 바꿀 때, send는 간접목적어 앞에 전치사 to가 필요하고 buy는 for가 필요하다.

Chapter 2
Be 동사와 일반동사

❶ Be 동사의 현재형

Pop Quiz → p. 26

1. are	2. are
3. Is	4. are
5. Are	6. is
7. is	8. am
9. is	10. Am

❷ 일반동사의 현재형

Pop Quiz → p. 27

1. is	2. Does
3. carries	4. have
5. don't	6. fixes
7. know	8. is
9. washes	10. does

Grammar Practice → p. 28

A

1. have	2. looks
3. Does	4. Are
5. has	

B

1. is	2. Do, like
3. doesn't go / does not go	4. am not
5. hurries	6. Is
7. Do, understand	8. seems
9. don't have / do not have	10. matches

C

1. don't look	2. love
3. Do, find	4. costs
5. doesn't clean	

❸ Be 동사의 과거형

❹ 규칙 동사의 과거형

Pop Quiz → p. 29

🖉
1. liked
2. carried
3. dropped
4. happened
5. helped
6. enjoyed
7. solved
8. decided
9. used
10. seemed
11. kicked
12. waited
13. changed
14. showed
15. died
16. visited
17. tied
18. reached
19. stayed
20. watched
21. lived
22. studied
23. shopped
24. looked
25. knitted
26. tasted

❺ 불규칙 동사의 과거형과 과거분사형

Pop Quiz → p. 30

🖉
1. forgot, forgotten
2. heard, heard
3. wrote, written
4. knew, known
5. drove, driven
6. became, become
7. let, let
8. caught, caught
9. left, left
10. thought, thought
11. sent, sent
12. brought, brought
13. took, taken
14. flew, flown

Grammar Practice → p. 31

A
1. tried
2. was
3. swam
4. left
5. stopped

B
1. were
2. hid
3. flew
4. walked
5. forgot

C
1. goed → went
2. was → were
3. begins → began
4. costed → cost
5. spoken → spoke

D
1. were
2. found
3. washed
4. cried
5. became

내신 대비 실전문제 → pp. 32-35

선택형

1. ②	2. ⑤	3. ③	4. ④	5. ①
6. ①	7. ②	8. ⑤	9. ③	10. ①
11. ②	12. ①	13. ③	14. ④	15. ②
16. ①	17. ③	18. ④	19. ③	20. ③

서술형

21. doesn't
22. ⑤, Nick ran into the house.
23. I am not from a small town.
24. Was Shelly busy
25. Is your chair comfortable?
26. has
27. The cafeteria food was not tasty.
28. The plane left on time.

고난도 서술형

29. doesn't speak any foreign languages
30. (1) I just stayed home and watched TV on Saturday. / I just watched TV at home on Saturday.
    (2) What did you do

[문제풀이]

선택형

1. 주어가 3인칭 단수 명사이고 시제가 현재(now)이므로 be 동사의 3인칭 단수 현재형인 is를 써야 한다.
2. make money ("돈을 벌다"); 주어가 I일 때 일반동사의 부정형에는 don't를 써야 한다; 주어가 this shirt일 때 일반동사의 의문문은 Does로 시작한다.
3. 주어가 Pizza and spaghetti이므로 동사는 복수형 aren't를 써야 한다.
4. ① → Is he a good student?
   ② → Ned is not polite.
   ③ → Are the tickets in your bag?
   ⑤ → The subway isn't crowded today.
5. ① bury → buries
6. ①은 동사가 둘(is need) 있어서 틀린 문장이다. 동사를 needs로 고쳐야 한다.

7. 주어인 Brad가 3인칭 단수이므로 Does Brad ~로 시작해야 한다.

8. 동사가 are이므로 3인칭 단수인 He는 주어가 될 수 없다.

9. goes가 3인칭 단수 현재형 동사이므로 부정문에는 doesn't go를 쓴다.

10. mean("의미하다")의 과거형은 meant이다.

11. My hair가 3인칭 단수이므로 뒤에 is/was가 와야 하고 Billy and Joe는 복수이므로 are/were가 올 수 있는데, 뒤에 과거를 뜻하는 five years ago와 last weekend가 있으므로 was, were가 맞다.

12. ② → Was that movie a big success?
    ③ → Was it really cold this morning?
    ④ → Wasn't Steve ready for the exam?
    ⑤ → Were we late for science class?

13. 문장의 주어가 각각 Pete, you, My new shoes이므로 어울리는 동사는 was, Were, weren't이다.

14. tap("두드리다")의 과거형은 tapped이다.

15. 동사가 was이므로 복수인 Red backpacks는 주어가 될 수 없다.

16. Everyone은 단수 취급하므로 동사 enjoy를 쓸 수 없고, 뒤에 last night이 있기 때문에 동사는 과거형 인 enjoyed를 써야 한다.

17. 주어가 you이고 시제가 과거이므로 Were을 써야 한다. 시점이 과거인 last Monday이므로 동사는 과거형인 assigned를 써야 한다.

18. sing("노래하다")의 과거형은 sang이다.

19. gotten은 동사의 과거형이 아니라 과거분사이다.

20. show("보여주다")의 과거형은 showed이다.

서술형

21. 주어가 모두 3인칭 단수이고 빈칸 뒤에 동사 원형이 있으므로 빈칸에는 일반동사의 3인칭 단수 부정형을 나타낼 때 필요한 doesn't를 써야 한다. usually나 on Sundays는 주로 현재시제에 쓰는 부사구다.

22. run("달리다")의 과거형은 ran이다.

23. be 동사의 1인칭 부정형은 am not이다.

24. 의문문이므로 be 동사인 was를 먼저 쓴 다음에 주어 Shelly를 쓴다.

25. 주어가 your chair이므로 동사는 Are가 아니라 Is를 쓴다.

26. 주어를 3인칭으로 바꾼 것이므로 동사도 has로 바꿔야 한다.

27. 동사 was의 부정형은 was not(=wasn't)이다.

28. 시제를 과거로 바꾸는 것이므로 동사를 과거형인 left 로 바꾼다.

고난도 서술형

29. speak은 일반동사이고 주어가 3인칭 단수이므로 부정형은 does not speak(= doesn't speak)을 쓴다.

30. (1) 토요일에 벌어진 일이므로 동사를 과거형으로 써야한다. 요일 앞에는 전치사 on을 쓴다.
    (2) 주어가 2인칭이고 의문사 what이 있는 의문문을 쓴다. 시제는 과거다.

Chapter 3
시제

❶ 현재 시제

Pop Quiz → p. 38

1. travels	2. are
3. doesn't teach	4. visit
5. grow	6. washes
7. is	8. knows
9. has	10. doesn't fall

❷ 과거 시제

Pop Quiz → p. 39

1. bought	2. planted
3. played	4. Did, begin
5. sang	6. were not / weren't
7. lost	8. would fight / fought
9. hit	10. used to have
11. Did, see	12. made
13. gave	14. didn't bring

❸ 미래 시제와 미래 시제 대용 표현

Pop Quiz → p. 40

A

1. graduate	2. leaving
3. won't be	4. see
5. starts	

B

1. will get
2. will be
3. invites
4. is going to fall
5. is opening / will open

Grammar Practice → p. 41

A

1. answers
2. is
3. live
4. lasts
5. keeps

B

1. enjoyed the movie last Friday
2. I broke my arm
3. was a famous pilot in the 1930s
4. used to have blond hair
5. ended 10,000 years ago

C

1. will help
2. begins
3. is
4. will invent
5. is going to die

D

1. saw the dentist six months ago
2. won't go out
3. arrives in Seoul
4. drives to work
5. burned/burnt the White House

❹ 현재분사와 현재진행

Pop Quiz → p. 42

A

1. calling
2. teaching
3. visiting
4. building
5. winning
6. standing
7. working
8. living
9. flying
10. sitting
11. talking
12. choosing
13. beginning
14. arriving
15. seeing

B

1. is taking
2. are sleeping
3. is falling
4. celebrating
5. cutting

❺ 과거진행

❻ 진행형으로 쓰지 않는 동사들

Pop Quiz → p. 43

A

1. were falling
2. were finishing
3. was taking
4. was staying
5. was shining

B

1. feels
2. are having
3. likes
4. looks
5. are enjoying

❼ 현재완료

Pop Quiz → p. 44

1. has been
2. has changed
3. Has, ever had
4. has never flown
5. have never heard
6. have happened
7. has lain
8. has never made
9. has improved
10. have been
11. Has, ever told
12. have, arrived

Grammar Practice → p. 45

A

1. hiking
2. playing
3. making
4. fighting
5. going

B

1. watching
2. waiting
3. closed
4. belonged
5. sounded

C

1. picked
2. seeing
3. owns
4. expecting
5. lied

D

1. have read
2. has just told
3. haven't chosen
4. has never learned
5. Have you ever met

내신 대비 실전문제 → pp. 46-49

선택형

1. ④	2. ②	3. ⑤	4. ①	5. ③
6. ①	7. ②	8. ⑤	9. ①	10. ③
11. ④	12. ⑤	13. ④	14. ①	15. ③
16. ⑤	17. ②	18. ①	19. ④	20. ⑤

서술형

21. seemed upset
22. ④, My parents have a new car.
23. (1) wrote, (2) is writing, (3) has written
24. Darla always cleans her room
25. has never lost a game
26. I haven't
27. The town used to be
28. Uncle Edward was telling a funny story.

고난도 서술형

29. (1) get, (2) got, (3) happened, (4) forgot
30. [예시 답안] Jane caught the ball /
The ball hit Jane, but she was OK /
Jane's friend caught the ball

[문제풀이]

선택형

1. 매일 저녁 반복되는 습관이므로 현재형을 써야 하고 주어가 3인칭 단수형이므로 ④ watches가 맞다.
2. ②에서 주어가 복수이므로 동사는 3인칭 단수형인 leads가 아니라 lead로 고쳐야 한다.
3. ① → Sandra wakes up early every day. (현재의 습관). ②, ③, ④도 주어가 3인칭 단수이므로 동사를 runs, doesn't have, likes로 바꾼다.
4. 5년 전에 일어난 일이므로 과거형 sold를 써야 한다.
5. yesterday나 last week과 같이 명확한 과거 표현이 있는 경우에는 동사의 과거형을 쓰는 것이 맞다.
   do the laundry: "세탁하다"
6. ① → Marianne hurt her arm a week ago.
   (명백한 과거)
7. ② → Ken and Eve are going to grow tomatoes.
8. will의 부정형은 will not(= won't)이다.
9. 시간을 나타내는 부사절에서는 현재 시제가 미래 시제

를 대신하므로 3인칭 단수 동사 ①이 맞다.

10. 〈단모음 + 단자음〉으로 끝나는 동사는 현재분사형을 만들 때 자음을 겹쳐 쓰고 -ing를 붙인다.
    ③ hiting → hitting
11. 현재의 습관이나 상황은 항상 현재 시제를 쓴다. 주어가 3인칭 단수이므로 ④ closes가 맞다.
12. 너(you)에게 묻는 말이므로 나(I)로 대답하며, be 동사의 현재형으로 묻는 문장이므로 be 동사 현재형으로 대답한 ⑤가 맞다.
13. ①, ②, ③, ⑤는 <be going to + 동사원형>으로 가까운 미래를 나타낸다. 이때 be going to는 will로 바꾸어 쓸 수 있다. ④는 go의 현재진행 시제로 가까운 미래를 나타낼 수도 있지만, will로 바꾸어 쓸 수 없다.
14. 과거 시점에 A가 전화했을 때 B가 무슨 일을 하고 있었는지를 답해야 하므로 과거진행 시제인 ①이 맞다.
15. be 동사가 있는 의문문은 주어와 be 동사의 순서만 바꾸면 된다.
    ① → Was the Sun shining?
    ② → Were we having fun?
    ④ → Was the pie baking in the oven?
    ⑤ → Was Grandma reading a story to us?
16. 과거의 경험을 표현하고 있으므로 현재완료 시제나 단순과거 시제를 사용한다.
    ⑤ was hearing → (has) heard
17. -e로 끝나는 동사의 현재분사형은 e를 생략하고 -ing를 붙인다. ② saveing → saving
18. 과거인 2010년에 시작되어 현재까지 계속되는 상황을 표현하고 있으므로 현재완료 시제 ①이 맞다.
19. ④ → catch – caught – caught
20. 현재완료 시제는 <have + 과거분사>이므로 과거형인 grew가 아닌 과거분사형 grown이 알맞다.

서술형

21. yesterday와 같이 명확한 과거를 나타내는 부사가 있을 경우 동사의 시제는 과거이므로 seemed upset을 써야 한다.
22. 소유를 나타내는 동사는 진행형을 쓰지 않는다.
23. 첫 번째 문장에는 명확한 과거를 나타내는 last year가 있으므로 wrote가 맞다. 두 번째 문장에는 now라는 현재를 알려주는 부사가 있으므로 현재 진행 중인 상황을 나타내는 현재진행 시제 is writing, 마지막 문장의 already와 어울리는 것은 현재완료 시제 has written이다.

24. 우선 문장에는 동사가 필요하고 그 앞에 주어가 오므로 Darla cleans로 시작할 수 있다. 빈도부사 always가 일반동사인 cleans 앞에 와서 Darla always cleans, 그 뒤에는 타동사인 clean의 목적어가 될 수 있는 her room이 온다.

25. 현재완료형 동사인 has lost를 사용하는 문제인데 빈도부사인 never가 그 사이에 들어간다. 그런 다음 목적어인 a game을 덧붙이면 된다.

26. Have로 시작하는 의문문에는 have를 사용하여 대답한다. No로 시작하기 때문에 부정으로 대답한다.

27. 지금과는 다른 과거의 상태를 나타내는 <used to + 동사원형>을 사용한다.

28. 과거진행으로 바꾸는 문제이므로, told를 was telling으로 바꾼다.

고난도 서술형

29. (1)에는 usually가 있는 것으로 보아 일반적인 사실을 나타내는 현재 시제가 필요하므로 get을 써야 한다. (2)에는 명백한 과거 표현 last week이 있으므로 got이 알맞다. (3)과 (4)에는 과거의 상황을 나타내는 happened, forgot을 써야 한다.

30. 공이 Jane을 향해 날아오는 상황이므로 그다음 행동을 상상하여 쓰면 된다. 과거 시제를 쓰는 것에 유의한다.

Chapter 4
명사와 관사

❶ 명사의 종류

Pop Quiz → p. 52

1. salt
2. a window
3. A dentist
4. a piece
5. homework
6. good advice
7. bottles

❷ 명사의 복수형

Pop Quiz → p. 53

1. ladies
2. boxes
3. elephants
4. fish
5. zoos
6. windows
7. thieves
8. bases
9. species
10. shrimp / shrimps
11. churches
12. women
13. mistakes
14. months
15. loaves
16. cities
17. computers
18. toys
19. mosquitoes
20. caps
21. trucks
22. feet
23. lambs
24. porches
25. days
26. fantasies
27. cloths
28. bosses
29. schools
30. toes

❸ 부정관사와 정관사

Pop Quiz → p. 54

1. a
2. an
3. Ø
4. the
5. The

Grammar Practice → p. 55

A
1. a bowl
2. a cup
3. a jar
4. two pieces
5. a glass

B
1. a university
2. the violin
3. golf
4. a month
5. dinner, the kitchen

C
1. give me a bottle of water
2. you like a slice of pie
3. ate two bowls of rice
4. used a jar of spaghetti sauce
5. forgot to buy a loaf of bread

D
1. Peace
2. The moon
3. an extra pencil
4. parties
5. series

내신 대비 실전문제 → pp. 56-59

선택형

1. ③	2. ①	3. ④	4. ①,④	5. ⑤
6. ③	7. ②	8. ③,④	9. ①	10. ①
11. ①	12. ②	13. ⑤	14. ④	15. ①
16. ⑤	17. ④	18. ②	19. ②	20. ③

서술형

21. ②, We were late because of traffic.
22. ③, People wear boots in the rain.
23. (1) a, (2) the
24. spoon, sentence, doll
25. shared a bowl of popcorn
26. children are playing on the grass
27. Mark will visit four cities on his trip.
28. This pair of shoes costs $30.

고난도 서술형

29. the man in the blue shirt
30. (1) an, (2) The, (3) a, (4) the

[문제풀이]

선택형

1. 동사 like의 목적어가 필요하므로 빈칸에 명사 형태가 와야 하고 관사가 없으므로 물질명사인 money가 적합하다. ①, ②, ④, ⑤는 모두 셀 수 있는 명사이므로 복수형으로 쓰거나 관사와 함께 써야 한다.
2. ① soda는 음료이므로 a bottle of soda, a glass of soda, a can of soda 등으로 써야 한다.
3. ④ → Alexandra has five uncles.
4. knowledge는 추상명사이고, snow는 물질명사이므로 셀 수 없는 명사다.
5. ⑤ holiday → holidays
6. 첫 번째 빈칸에는 빵을 세는 단위가 나와야 되므로 ②와 ④는 답이 될 수 없다. 두 번째 빈칸에는 설탕을 세는 단위가 와야 하므로 ⑤는 적절하지 않고, 세 번째 빈칸에 케이크를 세는 단위로 slice가 알맞기 때문에 ③이 답이다.
7. ② man → men
8. air, money는 둘 다 물질명사다.
9. ① party → parties
10. 고유명사 앞에는 관사를 붙이지 않으므로 ②에서는 the를 빼야 한다. 문맥상 다 알고 있는 대상을 가리키므로 ③에서는 Sky를 The sky로 고쳐야 한다. ④에서는 커피 한 잔을 뜻하므로 the를 a로 고쳐야

하며, ⑤에서는 특정한 자동차가 아니라 일반적인 자동차를 뜻하므로 정관사 the를 쓰지 않는다.
11. egg, airplane은 모음으로 시작하므로 앞에 부정관사 an이 와야 하고, movie 앞에는 부정관사 a가 온다.
12. ① → Nelly's favorite color is blue.
    ③ → Tony is taking a shower.
    ④ → Rabbits have soft fur.
    ⑤ → Don't eat fast food every day.
13. ⑤ belief → beliefs
14. ④ → Take a break if you're tired.
15. idea는 모음으로 시작하므로 앞에 부정관사 an을 써야 한다.
16. ① → Your toys are on the floor. (문맥상 누구나 알 수 있는 특정 대상)
    ② → Kindness is important. (추상명사 앞에 관사를 쓸 필요가 없다.)
    ③ → Aaron wears an orange scarf. (orange는 모음으로 시작하므로 앞에는 부정관사 an을 써야 한다.)
    ④ → This is a useful book. (useful의 첫 음은 모음이 아니라 반자음이므로 앞에는 부정관사 a를 써야 한다.)
17. ④ mouse의 복수형은 mice다.
18. ② lunch 앞에는 관사를 쓰지 않는다.
19. ① → The world has seven billion people.
    ③ → Teresa lives near an elementary school.
    ④ → We saw an elephant at the zoo.
    ⑤ → Yesterday we had an easy test.
20. pop music 앞에는 관사가 필요 없다.

서술형

21. traffic은 셀 수 없는 명사이므로 복수형으로 쓸 수 없다.
22. ③ boot → (a pair of) boots
23. 처음 언급되는 셀 수 있는 명사 앞에는 부정관사 a를 쓰고 다시 언급될 때는 정관사 the를 쓴다.
24. 보통명사인 spoon, sentence, doll은 셀 수 있는 명사다. cheese, water는 물질명사이며, honesty는 추상명사다.
25. popcorn을 세는 단위인 a bowl of를 이용해서 문장을 완성한다.
26. 주어를 복수형인 children으로 바꾸면 동사도 are playing으로 바꿔야 한다.

27. city의 복수는 cities다.

28. shoe는 짝을 이루는 명사이므로 복수형으로 쓴다.

고난도 서술형

29. 특정한 인물을 가리키므로 the man을 써야 하고, 보통명사 shirt 앞에 정관사 the를 써서 특정한 셔츠를 나타낸다.

30. (1)에는 excellent가 모음으로 시작하므로 an을 써야 하고, (2)에는 이미 언급된 lab을 가리키므로 정관사 the를 써야 한다. (3)에는 처음 언급되는 보통명사 library card 앞에 부정관사 a가 필요하고, (4)에는 이 상황에서 모두 알고 있는 대상을 가리키는 명사 front desk 앞에 정관사 the가 필요하다.

Chapter 5
대명사

❶ 인칭대명사

Pop Quiz → p. 62

1. she
2. his
3. their
4. him
5. yourself

❷ 지시대명사

❸ 비인칭 It

Pop Quiz → p. 63

A
1. those
2. that
3. These
4. this

B
1. 거리
2. 시간
3. 날씨

Grammar Practice → p. 64

A
1. they
2. myself
3. hers
4. our
5. them

B
1. This
2. these
3. Those
4. that
5. This

C
1. her
2. himself
3. yours
4. its
5. him

D
1. What time is it?
2. How far is it (from here)?
3. What's today's date? / What's the date today?
4. How's the weather (today)?
5. What day is it?

❹ 의문대명사

Pop Quiz → p. 65

1. What
2. Whose
3. Who(m)
4. Which
5. What
6. Who
7. Whose
8. Which

❺ 부정대명사

Pop Quiz → p. 66

1. anything
2. anyone
3. one
4. nothing
5. something
6. some
7. someone
8. Everyone
9. Nobody
10. everything

Grammar Practice → p. 67

A
1. anything / anyone
2. no one / nobody
3. any / anything
4. anything
5. one

B
1. What
2. Who
3. Who(m)
4. Whose
5. Which

C
1. something
2. Whose
3. Who
4. Which
5. anyone

D
1. Who(m) did you see at the festival?
2. Do you have anything/something to do right now?
3. Whose desk is that?
4. Is anyone/anybody/someone/somebody in the bathroom?
5. What is your favorite color?

내신 대비 실전문제 → pp. 68-71

선택형

1. ①	2. ④	3. ④	4. ②	5. ⑤
6. ②	7. ③	8. ①	9. ④	10. ③
11. ①	12. ⑤	13. ②	14. ③	15. ①
16. ④	17. ④	18. ③	19. ④	20. ②

서술형

21. Which
22. one
23. ④, Jamie knows something/someone famous.
24. (1) Our, (2) Your, (3) His
25. it
26. Who
27. something
28. her desk

고난도 서술형

29. (1) themselves, (2) myself, (3) ourselves
30. (1) My pencil case, (2) Heejin's

[문제풀이]

선택형

1. ① 주어 자리에는 주격을 써야 하므로 Us가 아니라 We가 알맞다.
2. ①, ②, ③에서 재귀대명사들은 모두 동사의 직접목적어로 쓰였고 ⑤에서는 전치사의 목적어로 쓰였기 때문에 생략할 수 없다. ④는 "직접, 스스로"라는 의미를 나타내는 강조의 재귀대명사이므로 생략 가능하다.
3. ④ his → him (목적격)

4. 첫 번째 빈칸에는 소유대명사인 ③ his와 ⑤ hers가 맞고, 두 번째 빈칸은 주어 자리이므로 주격인 ① She가 적합하다. 세 번째 빈칸은 주어 He를 강조하는 ⑤ himself가 들어갈 수 있다. ② her는 소유격이므로 뒤에 명사가 나와야 하는데 빈칸에는 소유격을 요구하는 자리가 없다.
5. 첫 번째 빈칸에는 동사 enjoy의 목적어가 나와야 하므로 주격으로 쓰인 ②와 ③은 답이 아니다. 두 번째 빈칸에는 소유대명사가 와야 하므로 주격인 ①과 목적격인 ④는 답이 아니다. 세 번째 빈칸은 주어 자리이므로 주격인 ⑤가 맞다.
6. ② Their → Its (The cat은 단수)
7. ③ your는 소유격이므로 뒤에 명사가 함께 나와야 빈칸에 들어갈 수 있다. 2인칭 소유대명사는 yours이다.
8. 단수명사 room을 수식하는 지시형용사인 ①이 알맞다.
9. 주어와 동사의 수를 일치시켜야 한다.
   ① → They/These/Those are my sunglasses.
   ② → This is good candy.
   ③ → Those were difficult questions.
   ⑤ → They were interesting speeches.
10. ③ That → Those
11. 첫 번째 빈칸에는 ice cream을 수식하는 말이 나와야하므로 단수인 this가 맞고, 두 번째 빈칸에는 복수 명사 two deer를 수식하는 말이 나와야 하므로 those가 맞다. 세 번째 빈칸에는 복수형 명사가 주어가 되어야 하므로 These가 맞다.
12. 〈소유격 + 명사〉는 소유대명사로 바꿀 수 있기 때문에 ⑤가 아니다. him은 목적격이다.
13. It이 인칭대명사로 쓰인 ②를 제외한 나머지는 모두 날씨, 시간, 거리를 나타내는 비인칭 주어로 쓰였다.
14. This로 물어보면 It으로 대답하기 때문에 답은 ③이다.
15. 책의 제목을 묻는 의문대명사가 필요하므로 답은 ①이다.
16. Whom은 목적격을 나타내는 의문대명사이고, Andrea가 좋아하는 사람을 묻고 있다.
17. 첫 번째 빈칸에는 부정문에 쓰이는 anything이 알맞다. 두 번째 빈칸에는 someone이나 anyone이 올 수 있다. 세 번째 빈칸에는 권유하는 의미의 something이 적합하다.
18. ③은 앞에 나온 명사를 대신 받는 부정대명사 one이고, 나머지는 여러 개 중 하나를 뜻하는 one이다.

19. ① → Everyone is here.
  ② → Somebody/Nobody made a mess.
  ③ → I'd like to talk to everyone.
  ⑤ → We hear someone talking.
20. 첫 번째 빈칸에는 의문문에 쓰이는 부정대명사 anything이 필요하고, 두 번째 빈칸에는 긍정문에 쓰이는 부정대명사 Someone, 세 번째 빈칸에는 전체부정을 뜻하는 nobody가 주어로 적합하므로 ②가 답이다.

서술형

21. 선택의문문이므로 Which로 묻는다.
22. 앞에 나온 명사 shirt를 대신 받는 부정대명사는 one이다.
23. ④에서는 know의 목적어로 명사나 대명사가 필요한데, any는 명사를 꾸미는 형용사 역할을 하므로 적절하지 않다.
24. 소유격의 알맞은 형태를 묻는 문제이다.
  We – Our, You – Your, He – His
25. 날씨, 시간, 날짜 등을 나타내는 비인칭 It이 필요하다.
26. 사람의 이름으로 대답한 것으로 보아 의문대명사 Who로 묻는 말이다.
27. 구체적인 일이 아니라 막연하게 relaxing한 일을 할 것이라는 의미에서 something을 쓰는 게 맞다.
28. 소유대명사는 〈소유격 + 명사〉이므로 이 문장에서 hers는 her desk를 가리킨다.

고난도 서술형

29. 적절한 재귀대명사를 써야 한다. Cats는 3인칭 복수이므로 themselves, I는 1인칭 단수이므로 myself, We는 1인칭 복수이므로 ourselves가 알맞다.
30. (1)의 소유대명사 Mine은 문맥으로 보아 my pencil case를 가리키며, (2)의 her는 바로 앞에 나온 Heejin's를 뜻한다.

Chapter 6
형용사와 부사

❶ 형용사의 기본 용법

❷ 수량 형용사

Pop Quiz → p. 74

A
1. famous, (한정적 용법)
2. heavy, (서술적 용법)
3. cold, (서술적 용법)
4. beautiful, (서술적 용법)

B
1. some, (수)
2. few, (수)
3. a little, (양)
4. much, (양)
5. Most, (수)

❸ 형용사의 비교급과 최상급

Pop Quiz → p. 75

1. more dangerous, most dangerous
2. quicker, quickest
3. more common, most common / commoner, commonest
4. cleaner, cleanest
5. more painful, most painful
6. cheaper, cheapest
7. more useful, most useful
8. more beautiful, most beautiful
9. more rapid, most rapid
10. more comfortable, most comfortable
11. more difficult, most difficult
12. thinner, thinnest
13. shinier, shiniest
14. taller, tallest

❹ 형용사와 비교 구문

Pop Quiz → p. 76

1. not as/so fantastic
2. healthier
3. more outgoing
4. not more enjoyable
5. far happier
6. even bigger
7. the most famous
8. not as fast
9. the most unique
10. funnier
11. the most delicious
12. not as challenging
13. better
14. the most exciting

Grammar Practice → p. 77

A

1. is
2. wear
3. are
4. hate
5. falls

B

1. is an excellent artist
2. makes him tired
3. finds Chinese difficult
4. sells a lot of nice clothes
5. needs a little salt

C

1. larger
2. the friendliest
3. as/so messy
4. more interesting
5. the most popular

D

1. as hardworking as
2. the loveliest
3. more exciting than
4. as/so shy as
5. the most frightening

❺ 부사의 형태

Pop Quiz → p. 78

A

1. incorrectly
2. enthusiastically
3. sadly
4. shyly
5. beautifully
6. creatively
7. quickly
8. luckily
9. carefully
10. historically

B

1. hard
2. late
3. early
4. fast
5. early

❻ 부사의 역할

❼ 빈도부사

Pop Quiz → p. 79

1. Dinner is <u>usually</u> served with wine.
2. Jenny can <u>often</u> be seen in the cafeteria.
3. You could <u>always</u> depend on me to help you out.

4. Jimmy <u>hardly ever</u> visits his parents during the school year.

❽ 부사구와 부사절

Pop Quiz → p. 80

1. to cash a check, 수표를 현금으로 바꾸기 위해
2. for a long time, 오랫동안
3. in order to avoid the traffic jam, 교통체증을 피하기 위해
4. at the gym, 체육관에서
5. under the kitchen sink, 부엌 싱크대 밑에
6. until I fell asleep, 내가 잠들 때까지
7. because he is shy, 그가 수줍기 때문에
8. If you save money, 네가 돈을 절약하면
9. Although whales look like fish, 고래는 물고기처럼 보이지만
10. because he didn't want to talk to his mother, 왜냐하면 그는 엄마에게 말하고 싶지 않았기 때문에

Grammar Practice → p. 81

A

1. beautifully
2. new
3. quietly
4. awful
5. correctly

B

1. in the kitchen
2. to buy a car
3. to see a lion
4. really/very loudly
5. on Friday afternoon(s)

C

1. <u>plays seldom</u> → seldom plays
2. <u>went to bed sometimes</u> → sometimes went to bed
3. <u>Hardly ever teenagers</u> → Teenagers hardly ever
4. <u>Never there is</u> → There is never
5. <u>be always</u> → always be

D

1. is often
2. sometimes gives
3. is usually
4. hardly ever smiles
5. has never won

선택형

1. ③	2. ⑤	3. ①	4. ②	5. ③
6. ②	7. ④	8. ③	9. ⑤	10. ⑤
11. ①	12. ④	13. ②	14. ④	15. ②
16. ①	17. ⑤	18. ②	19. ②	20. ④

서술형

21. ②, Most bottled water is cheap.
22. (1) as, (2) than, (3) the
23. I usually go to the market with my parents.
24. Nina is trying to correct all the mistakes in her essay.
25. closer/nearer than
26. internationally
27. early
28. Derek is never bored in science class.

고난도 서술형

29. (1) smarter, (2) funnier, (3) more outgoing
30. (1) more popular, (2) as popular,
    (3) the most popular

[문제풀이]

선택형

1. yellow는 명사를 수식하는 형용사이므로 sweater 앞에 쓸 수 있다.
2. ⑤ → I made the spicy soup.
3. a few ("몇 개의")
4. few는 수를 나타내므로 셀 수 없는 명사인 homework를 수식하지 못한다.
5. far는 비교급 강조 부사이므로 비교급 앞인 ③에 오는 것이 적절하다.
6. ② → modern – more modern – the most modern
7. 첫 번째 빈칸에는 비교의 대상이 없으므로 비교급이나 최상급이 나오지 않으므로 답은 ②와 ④ 중에 하나이다. 두 번째 빈칸 뒤에는 than이 있으며 빈칸에는 비교급이 와야 하므로 ④가 정답이다.
8. of the year라는 표현으로 보아 최상급이 나온다는 것을 알 수 있으므로 ③ the rainiest가 답이다.
9. ① the thinner → the thinnest
   ② more ugly → uglier
   ③ the tastier → the tastiest
   ④ bright → brighter
10. ⑤ → dirty – dirtier – the dirtiest

11. 원급 비교 구문의 어순은 <as + 형용사/부사 + as>이므로 ① intelligent가 맞다.
12. ④ very는 비교급을 강조하는 부사로 쓰지 않는다.
13. 동사를 수식하는 부사가 올 자리인데 ② lovely는 형용사이다.
14. ④ friend – friendly는 명사 – 형용사이고 나머지는 모두 형용사 – 부사이다.
15. 첫 번째 빈칸에는 동사 work를 수식하는 부사 hard가 필요하므로 ①과 ④는 답이 아니다. 두 번째 빈칸에는 목적어 most people의 상태를 나타내는 목적격보어 형용사가 필요하다. 세 번째 빈칸에는 동사를 수식하는 부사가 필요하므로 답은 ②다.
16. 빈칸에는 동사를 수식하는 부사나 부사구가 필요하므로 형용사인 ① wonderful은 적절하지 않다.
17. very는 부사를 수식하는 부사이므로 부사 앞에 온다. 따라서 recently 앞인 ⑤가 맞다.
18. How often은 빈도를 묻는 말이므로 빈도를 나타내는 부사로 대답해야 한다. 따라서 속도를 나타내는 부사 quickly는 대답이 될 수 없다.
19. ② <be afraid to + 동사원형> 은 "~하는 것이 마음 내키지 않다"는 뜻이다.
20. always는 빈도부사로 be 동사 뒤에 위치하므로 ④가 맞다.

서술형

21. water는 셀 수 없는 명사로 단수형이므로 동사도 단수형으로 써야 한다.
22. 첫 번째 빈칸은 <as + 형용사 + as>의 원급 비교이므로 as가 와야 한다. 두 번째 빈칸 앞에 비교급 형용사가 있으므로 빈칸에는 than이 적합하다. 세 번째 빈칸에는 최상급 앞에 쓰는 정관사가 필요하다.
23. usually는 빈도부사로 일반동사 앞에 위치한다.
24. mistake는 셀 수 있는 명사이므로 all the 뒤에서는 복수형인 mistakes로 써야 한다.
25. 빈칸에는 <형용사의 비교급 + than>이 와야 하므로 closer/nearer than이 알맞다.
26. travels를 수식하는 부사가 와야 하므로 internationally로 고쳐야 한다.
27. arrived를 수식하는 부사가 필요하다. early는 형용사와 부사의 형태가 같다.
28. "지루해한다"는 의미의 형용사는 bored이며, 빈도부사 never가 be 동사 뒤에 와야 한다.

29. 현우와 재민을 비교하는 글로, 현우가 재민보다 똑똑하고 재미있지만 재민만큼 외향적이지는 않다는 내용이다. 빈칸 뒤에 모두 than이 있으므로 빈칸에는 모두 비교급을 써야 한다.

30. (1)에서는 빈칸 뒤에 than이 있으므로 빈칸에 비교급이 와야 한다. (2)에서는 빈칸 뒤에 as가 있는 것으로 보아 빈칸에 원급 비교 구문에 쓰는 <as + 형용사>를 써야 한다. (3)에서는 of the four가 뒤에 오기 때문에 빈칸에 최상급 표현을 써야 한다.

Chapter 7
조동사

❶ 조동사의 종류와 기본 용법

Pop Quiz → p. 88

1. can	2. Do
3. will	4. was
5. Have	6. may
7. was	8. has

❷ 법조동사의 쓰임새

Pop Quiz → p. 89

1. Can we live to be one hundred?
2. May I use the Internet for a while?
3. There might not be ice cream for dessert.
4. Wouldn't you like to take a walk before dinner?
5. Sungmin doesn't have to take the exam again.

❸ 법조동사의 종류 Ⅰ

❹ 법조동사의 종류 Ⅱ

Pop Quiz → p. 90

1. can	2. could
3. was	4. might
5. be able to	6. can't
7. had better	8. would

Grammar Practice → p. 91

A

1. Did	2. is
3. can	4. does
5. Have	

B

1. must	2. might / may
3. doesn't have to	4. can't / must not
5. should / had better	

C

1. skate	2. have
3. won't	4. were able to
5. can	

D

1. mustn't borrow / can't borrow
2. will be able to make
3. must return / has to return
4. were able to find / could find
5. should try

내신 대비 실전문제 → pp. 92-95

1. ⑤	2. ③	3. ⑤	4. ③	5. ①
6. ①	7. ②	8. ③	9. ④	10. ②
11. ②	12. ⑤	13. ③	14. ①	15. ④
16. ④	17. ③	18. ①	19. ②	20. ①

21. Would the city have a festival
22. had to
23. will be able to live
24. (1) Are, (2) has
25. Will Josie or Billy give the presentation?
26. should
27. What does Craig have to do today?
28. wasn't able

29. You had better put the milk in the refrigerator.
30. (1) doesn't, (2) should, (3) will

선택형

1. for ten years라는 표현이 있으므로 lived 앞에 has를 써서 현재완료 시제를 나타낸다.

2. ① Will you lending → Will you lend
   ② aren't have → don't have
   ④ I'll → I'm
   ⑤ should use not → should not use

3. 주어가 3인칭 단수인 Matthew이므로 have to를 has to로 바꿔야 맞다.

4. ③ → We don't have to cook dinner tonight.

5. 첫 번째 빈칸에는 뒤에 yesterday라는 명확한 과거를 나타내는 부사가 있으므로 Did가 필요하다. 두 번째 빈칸에는 since 1999라는 표현이 있으므로 현재완료를 써야 한다.

6. 조동사 뒤에는 동사원형을 써야 한다.

7. ② can't는 금지의 의미를 나타내고 나머지는 모두 "~할 수 없다"는 능력의 의미를 나타낸다.

8. be 동사 다음에는 동사원형을 쓸 수 없다.

9. ④ → Dogs don't eat chocolate.

10. Maybe Natalia will은 미래에 일어날 가능성을 추측하는 것이므로 ② might로 바꾸어 쓸 수 있다.

11. 세 문장의 주어가 복수형, 1인칭, 2인칭이므로 ③과 ⑤는 답이 될 수 없다. 빈칸 모두 "~해야 한다"는 의미의 ② have to가 적절하다.

12. "꼭 필요한가?"라는 물음에 대한 부정적인 대답은 "~할 필요가 없다"이므로 ⑤가 적절하다.

13. 주말 계획을 제안하고 있으므로 빈칸에는 Shall이 적합하다.

14. <had better + 동사원형>은 "~하는 게 낫다"는 뜻으로, 부정형은 <had better not + 동사원형>이다.

15. 첫 번째 문장에서는 부탁의 의미이므로 Would 대신 Will이나 Can을 쓸 수 있고, 두 번째 문장에서는 미래를 나타내므로 will로 바꾸어 쓸 수 있다.

16. should는 "~해야 한다"는 뜻이므로 과거 시제에 어울리지 않는다.

17. might not은 금지의 의미가 아니라 추측의 의미로 쓰인다.

18. a, b는 추측의 의미를 나타내고, c, d, e는 금지의 의미를 나타낸다.

19. ②에서 두 번째 문장에 근거가 제시되어 있으므로 빈칸에는 확신을 나타내는 must를 써야 한다.

20. 첫 번째 빈칸에는 필요를 나타내는 조동사 must, have to가 알맞고, 두 번째 빈칸에는 추측을 나타내는 can, might, should가 적합하다. 세 번째 빈칸에는 추측을 나타내는 might not이 알맞기 때문에 정답은 ①이다.

서술형

21. 조동사가 있는 문장의 의문문은 조동사와 주어의 위치만 바꾸면 된다.

22. "~해야 했다"라는 과거의 필요를 나타낼 때 had to를 쓴다.

23. 미래의 가능성을 나타내는 표현이므로 조동사 will 뒤에 be able to가 온다.

24. (1)에는 뒤에 now가 있으므로 현재진행 시제를 나타내기 위해 Are가 필요하다. (2)에는 부사 already가 있고 그 앞에 ended가 있는 것으로 보아 직전에 완료된 행동을 나타내기 위해 현재완료 시제를 써야 하므로 has가 필요하다.

25. 조동사가 있는 의문문이므로 주어 뒤에 동사원형을 써야 한다.

26. 두 가지 가운데 하나를 제안하는 것이므로 조동사 should가 적합하다.

27. 의문사가 있는 의문문을 완성해야 하므로 의문사 what을 먼저 쓰고, "~을 해야 한다"는 의미를 나타내는 조동사 have to를 의문문에 맞게 사용하여 완성한다.

28. "~을 할 수 없었다"는 의미를 나타내는 couldn't는 wasn't able to로 바꿔 쓸 수 있다.

고난도 서술형

29. "~하는 게 좋겠다"는 의미의 <had better + 동사원형>을 이용해서 완성한다.

30. 문맥상 다정하게 대해주지 않는 언니에 관한 조언을 구하는 내용이므로 (1)에는 현재의 습관적인 행위를 나타내는 현재 시제를 쓰는 것이 적합하므로 doesn't가 어울리고, (2)에는 "어떻게 하는 게 좋죠?" 하고 묻고 있으므로 조동사 should가 알맞다. (3)에는 앞에 In a few years라는 미래를 나타내는 표현이 있으므로 조동사 will이 어울린다.

Chapter 8
수동태

❶ 수동태의 쓰임새

Pop Quiz → p. 98

1. was completed
2. are attacking
3. is taught
4. is done
5. traveled

❷ 수동태 문장 만들기

Pop Quiz → p. 99

A
1. were killed
2. was seen
3. are enjoyed
4. is spoken
5. are held

B
1. is hated
2. were written
3. was not made
4. are sold
5. are sent

❸ 수동태의 시제

Pop Quiz → p. 100

1. will be given / are going to be given
2. have been chosen
3. was elected
4. was not built
5. have not been found
6. were trained

Grammar Practice → p. 101

A
1. was created
2. are expected
3. has been arrested
4. started
5. being repaired

B
1. was sung by the Beatles
2. are made by many companies
3. am rarely beaten by my sister
4. were taken by a famous artist
5. were destroyed by the earthquake
6. has been viewed by millions of Internet users
7. will not be read by other people / is not going to be read by other people
8. has not been examined by the doctor
9. will be hosted by Russia / is going to be hosted by Russia
10. was not being taught by Mr. Yoo

C
1. are grown
2. will be given / are going to be given
3. hasn't been cleaned
4. are watched
5. was invented

내신 대비 실전문제 → pp. 102-105

선택형

1. ⑤	2. ②	3. ③	4. ④	5. ②
6. ①	7. ⑤	8. ⑤	9. ⑤	10. ①
11. ②	12. ①	13. ③	14. ④	15. ①
16. ②	17. ③	18. ④	19. ③	20. ①

서술형

21. not been made
22. will be held
23. Were
24. ④ stole → was stolen
25. hasn't been
26. are grown by my mom
27. Kim and Joseph aren't going to be invited to the part.
28. All the concert tickets have been sold.

고난도 서술형

29. A local artist was using the basement as a workshop.
30. flight has been delayed by bad weather

[문제풀이]

선택형

1. 수동태 문장은 <be 동사 + 과거분사>의 형태다.
2. 원래 문장의 목적어인 French fries가 주어가 되고 동사가 <be 동사 + 과거분사>의 형태로 된 ②가 답이다.

3. be 동사 뒤에 올 수 있는 동사의 형태는 현재분사(-ing)와 과거분사인데 현재분사를 쓰면 진행 시제가 되고 과거분사를 쓰면 수동태가 된다.

4. 주어가 3인칭 단수이므로 is가 맞다.

5. seem은 상태를 나타내는 자동사이기 때문에 수동태 문장에는 쓰이지 않는다.
   ② → Lena seemed happy with her gift.

6. 미래 문장의 수동태는 <will be + 과거분사>의 형태다.

7. 현재완료 수동태(has/have been + 과거분사) 문장을 의문문으로 나타낸 것으로 조동사 has와 주어가 앞으로 나가고 been taken이 남은 형태다.

8. 과거 시제 수동태이며, "태어났다"는 의미를 나타낼 때 항상 was/were born을 쓴다.

9. ⑤ → Smart phones are often used for email.

10. 과거 시제로 쓰면 was built도 되지만, 완료된 사실을 강조하기 위해 현재완료 수동태인 has been built로 쓸 수 있다.

11. 수동태 문장을 완성하기 위해 빈칸에 과거분사가 필요하다.

12. ① → Egypt is known for its amazing pyramids.

13. "취소될 것이다"라는 의미를 나타내기 위해 is going to 뒤에 수동태 형식이 필요하다.

14. 주어가 단수이고 문맥상 부정형이 필요하다. won't나 doesn't 뒤에는 반드시 동사원형이 와야 하므로 여기에 쓸 수 없다. hasn't를 써서 현재완료 수동태를 완성하면 된다.

15. been 뒤에 올 수 있는 동사의 형태는 과거분사 cut밖에 없다.

16. 주어가 복수이고 타동사 marry, take를 이용하여 상태를 나타내야 하므로 수동태 표현이 필요하다. 첫 번째 문장에 for ten years가 있으므로 현재완료 시제를 써서 <have been + 과거분사>의 형태로 나타낸다.

17. <by + 행위자>가 뒤에 오는 것으로 보아 첫 번째 빈칸에는 수동태 형식이 필요하다. 두 번째 빈칸이 있는 문장은 I가 주어이고 목적어 my friend도 있으므로 수동태 형식으로 쓰지 않는다. 따라서 ③이 답이다.

18. ① → Many accidents occur/occurred on the highway. (occur는 자동사)
    ② → Some money was taken from Jen's bag.
    ③ → Several students will be given awards.

⑤ → Your computer hasn't been fixed yet.

19. 첫 번째 빈칸에는 앞에 행위자가 있으므로 능동태인 tore가 알맞다. 두 번째, 세 번째 문장은 수동태 형식이 필요한데, 두 번째 문장은 현재완료 수동태, 세 번째 문장은 과거 수동태로 완성한다.

20. 실내화(slippers)를 주어로 하여 수동태 문장을 완성한다. 빈도부사 usually는 be 동사 뒤에 위치한다.

21. has made를 수동태 부정형으로 바꾸면 has not been made가 맞다.

22. hold가 타동사이고 주어가 사람이 아니라 모임이다. 따라서 수동태 형식이 필요하며, 미래 시제로 써야 한다.

23. 과거분사 woken과 행위자를 나타내는 전치사 by가 있는 것으로 보아 수동태 문장이므로 Have를 Were로 고쳐야 한다.

24. 행위 대상인 그림 Mona Lisa가 주어이므로 동사를 수동태 형식인 was stolen으로 바꿔야 한다.

25. 단수명사인 A bear는 보는 행위의 대상이므로 수동태 형식이 있어야 한다. since 절이 뒤에 오기 때문에 현재완료 시제인 <hasn't been + 과거분사>로 써야 한다.

26. 현재 시제의 수동태로 변환한다.

27. be going to 뒤에는 동사원형을 써야 하는데 invited가 와서 틀렸다. 주어인 Kim and Joseph이 파티에 초대받은 대상이므로 동사의 형태가 수동태가 되어야 한다.

28. 주어가 될 수 있는 명사가 concert tickets밖에 없으므로 수동태 문장으로 써야 한다. All the는 명사를 수식하므로 concert tickets 앞에 쓰고, 남은 세 단어로 수동태 형식을 완성하면 have been sold가 맞다.

29. 동사가 was being used이므로 과거진행 문장으로 변환하면 된다.

30. 주어진 단어들 가운데 been이 있는 것으로 보아 수동태 문장이 필요함을 알 수 있다. 주어로는 The flight이 적합하며, bad weather는 사건의 원인(즉 행위자)일 것이다. 동사의 형태는 has been delayed가 된다.

Chapter 9
부정사

❶ 명사 역할을 하는 To 부정사

Pop Quiz → p. 108

1. to visit	2. to finish
3. To be	4. to work
5. to stay	6. to become
7. to pay	

❷ 형용사 역할을 하는 To 부정사

Pop Quiz → p. 109

1. a different topic to research
2. anything good to watch on TV
3. easy way to get important vitamins
4. nothing to worry about
5. about time to turn on the heater
6. a chance to see her cousins
7. anything to do in his free time

❸ 부사 역할을 하는 To 부정사

❹ 원형부정사

Pop Quiz → p. 110

1. to swim	2. steal
3. play	4. to score
5. to be	6. to keep
7. fall	8. start
9. to understand	10. to give

Grammar Practice → p. 111

A

1. to allow	2. stay
3. to get	4. to build
5. shake	

B

1. Dana decided to tell everyone the truth.
2. What is the fastest way to get downtown?
3. We all felt very relieved to see the plane land safely.
4. It is rude to chew food with your mouth open.
5. Let's think of something fun to do this weekend.

C

1. to buy	2. give
3. to finish	4. say
5. to see	

D

1. takes a lot of time to learn
2. agreed not to fight
3. one more exam to take
4. to make a new friend
5. live to be 100 years old

내신 대비 실전문제 → pp. 112-115

선택형

1. ③	2. ③	3. ④	4. ④	5. ⑤
6. ②	7. ①	8. ⑤	9. ④	10. ②
11. ④	12. ①	13. ②	14. ⑤	15. ⑤
16. ②	17. ④	18. ①	19. ③	20. ③

서술형

21. not to buy a new car
22. a way to improve her grades
23. ①, I hate riding/to ride on a crowded subway.
24. to say *thank you*
25. to join
26. Roberta promised not to be late for practice.
27. to rest
28. decision to buy a motorcycle

고난도 서술형

29. (some) new clothes to wear
30. [예시 답안] they asked the man/him to be quiet

[문제풀이]

선택형

1. need(s) to: "~할 필요가 있다"
2. write는 동사이므로 be 동사 뒤 보어 자리에 쓸 수 없다. 명사나 형용사가 보어가 될 수 있는데, 여기서는

"~하는 것"이라는 의미의 명사 보어가 필요하다. 따라서 ③ write를 to write로 바꾸어야 한다.

3. ④의 to 부정사는 형용사를 수식하는 부사적 용법인데, 나머지는 모두 명사를 수식하는 형용사적 용법이다. ①과 ③은 to 부정사 앞에 형용사가 있는데, 그 형용사들도 모두 앞에 있는 someone, anywhere를 수식한다는 점에 유의한다.

4. ④를 제외한 모든 문장의 to 부정사는 진주어로 쓰였는데, ④의 to 부정사는 앞에 있는 명사 time을 수식하는 형용사 역할을 한다.

5. It's about time to: "~할 시간이 거의 됐다"

6. 주어진 문장에서 to 부정사는 보어로 쓰였는데, ②의 to 부정사는 타동사의 목적어로 쓰였다.

7. ① → To make(= making) mistakes is human.

8. ⑤는 타동사 forget의 목적어로 쓰였는데, 나머지는 모두 앞에 있는 명사를 수식하는 형용사 역할을 한다.

9. ④의 to 부정사는 앞에 있는 명사를 수식하는 형용사로 쓰였고, 나머지 문장의 to 부정사는 모두 형용사를 수식하는 부사적 용법으로 쓰였다.

10. need 다음에 명사 목적어 somewhere가 나와야 하고 그 뒤에 이를 수식하는 형용사와 to 부정사가 오면 된다.

11. ④의 to look은 행위의 목적을 나타내는 부사적 용법으로 쓰였는데, 나머지 문장의 to 부정사는 모두 타동사의 목적어 역할을 하는 명사적 용법으로 쓰였다.

12. 주어진 문장의 to 부정사는 감정의 원인을 나타내는 부사적 용법으로 쓰였는데, ①의 to 부정사가 같은 용법으로 쓰였다. ②의 to 부정사는 목적을 나타내고, ③에서는 목적격보어로 쓰였으며, ④에서는 형용사를 수식하고, ⑤에서는 문장의 진주어로 쓰였다.

13. 명사 decision을 수식할 to 부정사가 필요하다.

14. 주어진 문장에서 to 부정사는 행위의 목적을 나타내는데, ⑤의 to 부정사가 같은 용법으로 쓰였다. ①에서는 감정의 원인, ②와 ③에서는 명사 수식, ④에서는 형용사 수식 용법으로 쓰였다.

15. 문맥상 행위의 목적을 나타내는 to 부정사가 필요하다.

16. hope는 to 부정사를 목적어로 취하는 동사이다. 나머지 동사들 make, let, watch, see는 뒤에 〈목적어 + 동사원형〉을 쓴다.

17. 앞에 있는 형용사를 수식하는 부사적 용법의 to 부정사를 찾는 문제로 ④가 정답이다. ①에서는

문장의 진주어로, ②에서는 명사를 수식하는 형용사적 용법으로, ③에서는 타동사의 목적어로, ⑤에서는 감정의 원인을 나타내는 용법으로 쓰였다.

18. allow 뒤에 〈목적어 + to 부정사〉가 와서 "[목적어]가 ~하는 것을 허락하다"는 의미를 나타낸다. 지각동사 listen to 뒤에는 〈목적어 + 동사원형/현재분사〉가 와서 "[목적어]가 ~하는 것을 듣다"는 의미를 나타낸다.

19. ① → Laura went to the theater to see a play.
    ② → I was angry to see the big mess.
    ④ → They never learned to play an instrument.
    ⑤ → It isn't unusual to get a cold in winter.

20. 사역동사 had 뒤에 〈목적어 + 동사원형〉을 써서 "[목적어]가 ~하게 시키다"는 의미를 나타낸다.

서술형

21. decide not to buy: "~을 사지 않기로 결정하다"

22. 타동사 find의 목적어인 a way를 먼저 쓰고 이를 수식하는 형용사 역할을 할 to 부정사구를 그 뒤에 이어서 쓴다.

23. I hate riding/to ride on a crowded subway. (riding 대신에 to ride를 쓰면 구체적인 상황, riding을 쓰면 일반적인 취향이나 선호)

24. It을 문장의 가주어로 쓰고 to 부정사구를 진주어로 쓸 수 있다.

25. allow 뒤에 〈목적어 + to 부정사〉가 와서 "[목적어]가 ~하는 것을 허락하다"는 의미를 나타낸다.

26. promise 뒤에 보통 to 부정사를 쓰지만 "~하지 않기로 약속하다"는 뜻을 나타내려면 to 부정사 앞에 not을 먼저 써서 promise not to be late의 순서로 써야 한다.

27. 행위의 목적을 나타내는 to 부정사를 이용하여 완성한다.

28. made a decision to: "~하기로 결심하다"

고난도 서술형

29. needs의 목적어인 "새 옷"(new clothes)을 먼저 쓴 다음 이를 수식할 to 부정사를 뒤에 이어 쓴다.

30. 주어진 단어가 asked, be, quiet이므로 그들(Lori and Mark)이 영화관에서 큰 목소리로 통화하는 사람에게 조용히 해달라고 요청할 것이다. ask 뒤에는 〈목적어 + to 부정사〉가 온다.

Chapter 10
동명사

❶ 동명사의 역할

Pop Quiz → p. 118

1. playing
2. Making
3. seeing
4. choosing
5. Collecting
6. inviting
7. reading

❷ 동명사와 현재분사

❸ 동명사와 To 부정사

Pop Quiz → p. 119

A
1. 동명사
2. 현재분사
3. 현재분사
4. 동명사

B
1. to live
2. drinking
3. to join
4. taking

❹ 동명사의 관용적 표현

Pop Quiz → p. 120

1. had trouble
2. spend a lot of time
3. how about
4. It's no use
5. can't help
6. I look forward to
7. goes

Grammar Practice → p. 121

A
1. listening
2. paying
3. Hunting
4. helping
5. waking up

B
1. in collecting
2. to join
3. taking
4. to buy
5. fixing

C
1. to swim / swimming
2. to turn off
3. speaking
4. lending
5. attending

D
1. going fishing
2. Drinking water
3. a lot of time exercising
4. catching/getting a cold
5. have trouble/difficulty reading

내신 대비 실전문제 → pp. 122-125

선택형

1. ④	2. ②	3. ①	4. ③	5. ③
6. ②	7. ①	8. ①	9. ②	10. ⑤
11. ③	12. ④	13. ③	14. ②	15. ②
16. ⑤	17. ③	18. ①	19. ②	20. ④

서술형

21. taking
22. couldn't help falling asleep
23. ④, How about going fishing next weekend?
24. living
25. The dog has difficulty walking on two legs.
26. (1) Taking, (2) to use
27. Do you remember meeting Jeff last summer?
28. sending

고난도 서술형

29. looking forward to turning
30. (1) biting, (2) covering, (3) to relax

[문제풀이]

선택형

1. 주어가 필요하므로 Give를 동명사 Giving으로 바꿔야 한다.
2. 전치사 at의 목적어로 동명사를 써야 한다.
3. ② → I forgot to tell you the news.
   ③ → The cats enjoy drinking milk.
   ④ → Do you want to go to sleep?
   ⑤ → Let's finish eating lunch.
4. ③의 동명사는 타동사의 목적어로 쓰였으며 나머지는 모두 문장의 주격보어로 쓰였다.
5. 문맥상 "~하기 위해 가던 길을 멈추다"는 의미이므로 행위의 목적을 나타내는 to have를 써야 한다.

6. ② → Jane practices hitting a baseball.
7. expect 뒤에는 흔히 to 부정사가 오고, start 뒤에는 to 부정사와 동명사 모두 올 수 있다.
8. 전치사 by 뒤에 동명사 being을 써야 한다.
9. 주어진 문장에서 crying은 명사를 수식하는 현재분사이다. ②의 falling이 같은 용법으로 쓰였으며 나머지는 모두 동명사로 쓰였다.
10. 첫 번째 문장에는 tomorrow가 뒤에 오기 때문에 미래의 일을 기억한다는 의미에서 forget 뒤에 to 부정사를 써야 한다. 두 번째 문장에는 주어가 필요하므로 명사 역할을 할 수 있는 동명사나 to 부정사가 필요하다. 동사원형은 주어가 될 수 없다.
11. regret은 과거에 대한 후회를 나타낼 때 동명사를 목적어로 취한다.
12. 주어진 문장에서 Exercising은 주어로 쓰인 동명사로, ④의 Taking이 같은 용법으로 쓰였다. 나머지 중 ①, ②, ⑤는 모두 뒤에 오는 명사를 수식하는 현재분사이며, ③은 명사로 쓰인 예이다.
13. 첫 번째 문장에서는 타동사의 목적어, 두 번째 문장에서는 전치사의 목적어로 동명사가 각각 필요하다.
14. 주어진 문장의 sleeping은 현재진행 시제를 나타내는 현재분사로, ②의 taking이 같은 용법으로 쓰였다. 나머지는 모두 주격보어로 쓰인 동명사다.
15. ① → go, ③ → seeing,
④ → to see, ⑤ → to pay
16. ⑤의 동명사는 전치사의 목적어로 쓰였으며 나머지는 모두 타동사의 목적어로 쓰였다.
17. doesn't 뒤에 일단 동사원형 spend를 써야 하며, 그 뒤에는 목적어를 쓴다. spend + 시간 + -ing: "~하는 데 시간을 보내다"
18. have trouble + -ing: "~하느라 애를 먹다"
19. mind는 동명사를 목적어로 취하는 타동사이다.
② → doing
20. look forward to + -ing: "~하기를 고대하다"
go + -ing: "~하러 가다"

21. try + -ing: "~을 한번 시도해 보다"
take an aspirin: "아스피린을 복용하다"
22. cannot/couldn't help + -ing:
"~하는 것을 참을 수 없다/없었다"
23. How about + -ing: "~하는 게 어때?"
24. 전치사 of 뒤에 동명사를 쓴다.

25. have difficulty + -ing: "~하느라 고생하다"
26. (1)에는 주어가 필요하므로 동명사 Taking을 써야 한다. (2)에는 형용사 safer를 수식할 수 있는 to 부정사가 필요하다.
27. 과거의 행위를 기억할 때에는 remember 뒤에 동명사를 쓴다.
28. enjoy는 동명사를 목적어로 취한다.

고난도 서술형
29. look forward to + -ing: "~하기를 고대하다"
30. (1) quit은 동명사를 목적어로 취하는 동사다.
(2) try + -ing: "~하는 것을 시도하다"
(3) remember 뒤에 to 부정사를 쓰면 미래의 의미가 되어 조언을 나타낸다.

Chapter 11
분사

❶ 분사의 개념과 종류

Pop Quiz → p. 128

1. boring
2. frozen
3. confusing
4. surprising
5. bottled

❷ 분사의 쓰임새

Pop Quiz → p. 129

1. leaving
2. grown
3. frightening
4. seen
5. called

❸ 분사와 To 부정사

❹ 분사와 동명사

Pop Quiz → p. 130

A
1. to get
2. broken
3. exciting
4. to write

B

1. 현재분사
2. 동명사
3. 동명사
4. 현재분사

Grammar Practice → p. 131

A

1. cheering
2. rising
3. met
4. confused
5. locked

B

1. disgusting
2. missed
3. made
4. playing
5. answered

C

1. All the tickets for the concert have been sold.
2. We're always so bored on rainy Sunday afternoons.
3. Bridget walked into the room smiling brightly.
4. Cooked noodles are very soft.
5. There are two people arguing in the hallway.

D

1. children to take care of
2. written by our teacher
3. Learning to drive
4. a flying mouse
5. playing in the rain

내신 대비 실전문제 → pp. 132-135

선택형

1. ③	2. ①	3. ⑤	4. ④	5. ②
6. ①	7. ④	8. ③	9. ①	10. ②
11. ④	12. ④	13. ⑤	14. ②	15. ②
16. ⑤	17. ③	18. ①	19. ③	20. ①

서술형

21. to finish
22. to help
23. ④, It was amazing to meet my favorite actress.
24. playing
25. Who is that handsome man talking to Dylan?
26. worn
27. Did Nathan find his lost wallet?
28. (1) decorated, (2) hanging

고난도 서술형

29. The smiling girl is eating fried chicken.
30. [예시 답안] (1) Charlie is very excited.
    (2) Many surprising things happen.
    (3) This book is never boring.

[문제풀이]

선택형

1. be interested in: "~에 흥미가 있다"
2. 주어진 문장은 현재진행을 나타내는 현재분사로, ①의 raining이 같은 용법으로 쓰였다. ②와 ⑤는 명사를 수식하는 형용사로 쓰였으며, ③과 ④는 주격보어로 쓰였다.
3. ⑤ frightened는 사람의 감정을 나타내는 형용사이므로 frightening으로 바꿔야 한다.
4. 명사를 수식하는 형용사가 필요한 자리인데, frying onions는 의미가 성립되지 않는다.
5. ②는 명사를 수식하는 형용사로 쓰인 과거분사이고, 나머지는 모두 현재완료 시제를 이루는 과거분사다.
6. 명사 rides를 수식하는 형용사가 필요한데, rides(탈것들)는 흥미를 주는 주체이므로 현재분사 exciting을 써야 한다.
7. 첫 번째 문장에는 수동태 형식을 이루는 과거분사가 필요하고, 두 번째 문장에는 과거진행을 나타내기 위해 현재분사가 필요하다.
8. 문맥상 피곤한 상태를 나타내야 하므로 과거분사 tired를 써야 한다.
9. a에서는 문장의 주어로 쓰인 동명사, c에서는 동명사의 관용적인 용법, e에서는 타동사의 목적어로 쓰인 동명사이며, b에서는 앞에 있는 명사를 수식하는 현재분사, d에서는 문장의 목적격보어로 쓰인 현재분사의 용법이다.
10. 첫 번째 문장에는 지각동사 hear 뒤에 목적격보어로 동사원형이나 현재분사가 필요하며, 두 번째 문장에는 수동태 형식을 완성하기 위해 과거분사가 필요하다.
11. ④의 eating은 과거진행을 나타내는 현재분사이며, ①의 Eating은 주어로 쓰인 동명사, ②, ⑤에서는 모두 타동사의 목적어로 쓰인 동명사이며, ③에서는 전치사의 목적어로 쓰인 동명사이다.
12. 첫 번째 문장에는 명사 fruit을 수식할 수 있는 형용사 dried(말린)가 필요하고, 두 번째 문장에는 과거완료를 만들기 위한 과거분사 dried가 필요하다.

13. ⑤의 sitting은 전치사의 목적어로 쓰인 동명사이고, ①, ③, ④는 앞에 있는 명사를 뒤에서 수식하는 형용사로 쓰였으며, ②에서는 문장의 목적격보어인 형용사 용법으로 쓰였다.
14. 주어진 문장에서 singing은 용도나 목적을 나타내는 동명사로 쓰였는데, ②의 taking만 동명사이고 (타동사의 목적어로 쓰였음), 나머지는 모두 현재분사이다.
15. ① → The class felt worried about the quiz.
    ③ → I'm confused about the meaning of this word.
    ④ → All the tickets have been sold already.
    ⑤ → Stores were closed for two days because of Chuseok.
16. a와 b는 동사의 과거형으로 쓰였고, c와 d는 앞에 있는 명사를 수식하는 과거분사이며, e는 수동태 형식을 이루는 과거분사이다.
17. ① → Would you like something to drink?
    ② → His favorite exercise is riding a bike.
    ④ → Everyone was laughing at the joke.
    ⑤ → I wore a frightening mask on Halloween.
18. 첫 번째 문장에는 anything을 뒤에서 수식하는 to 부정사를 써야 하며, 두 번째 문장에는 명사 girl을 뒤에서 수식할 수 있는 현재분사가 필요하다.
19. ① → coming, ② → baking,
    ④ → to make, ⑤ → trying
20. annoying ("짜증 나게 하는")

서술형

21. 명사 뒤에서 수식할 수 있는 to 부정사가 필요하다.
22. someone을 수식할 to 부정사가 필요하다.
23. amazed는 사람의 감정을 표현하는 형용사이며 여기서는 주어가 to meet my favorite actress 이므로 amazing을 써야 한다.
24. 명사 band를 뒤에서 수식할 수 있는 현재분사를 써야 한다.
25. 명사 man을 뒤에서 수식할 수 있는 현재분사 talking으로 고쳐야 한다.
26. 행위자 by가 빈칸 뒤에 있는 것으로 보아 앞에는 수동태 형식에서 〈관계대명사 + be 동사〉가 생략되고 남은 과거분사 worn을 쓰면 된다.
27. wallet 앞에 있는 losing을 "잃어버린"이라는 의미의 과거분사(형용사) lost로 고쳐야 한다.
28. (1)에는 침실의 상태를 나타내므로 과거분사 decorated가 알맞다. (2)에는 앞에 있는 명사 picture를 수식하는 현재분사가 필요하다.

고난도 서술형

29. 미소 짓는 소녀(the smiling girl) 먹고 있다(is eating)
30. (1)에는 사람의 감정 상태를 나타내기 위해 과거분사(형용사) excited가 필요하고, (2)에는 "놀라게 하는"이라는 능동 의미의 현재분사 surprising을 쓰는 게 적합하며, (3)에도 "지루하게 하는"이라는 의미의 현재분사 boring을 이용해서 문장을 완성한다.

Chapter 12
접속사와 전치사

❶ 등위접속사

Pop Quiz → p. 138

1. and
2. or
3. but
4. for
5. so
6. so
7. and
8. yet

❷ 종속접속사

❸ 접속부사

Pop Quiz → p. 139

A
1. when she was painting the ceiling, (시간)
2. because he is very friendly, (이유)
3. if you want, (조건)
4. Since Joseph is bad at card games, (이유)
5. Although the weather was not good, (양보)

B
1. Meanwhile
2. accordingly
3. Nonetheless
4. thus
5. Furthermore

Grammar Practice → p. 140

A
1. so
2. or
3. and
4. for
5. but

B

1. If
2. when
3. before
4. Because
5. Though

C

1. Thus / Therefore
2. however / nonetheless
3. moreover
4. Nonetheless / However
5. therefore / thus

D

1. before the library closes
2. although/though she wanted a puppy
3. while he's on the subway
4. if I go to bed at 2 a.m.
5. Furthermore/Moreover, they help a lot of people

❹ 전치사

Pop Quiz → p. 141

A

1. on
2. under
3. after
4. during

B

1. on
2. in
3. with
4. for

❺ 전치사의 관용적 표현

Pop Quiz → p. 142

A

1. of
2. for
3. to
4. with
5. in

B

1. it up
2. it off
3. off
4. by
5. for

Grammar Practice → p. 143

A

1. for
2. during
3. After
4. in
5. before

B

1. under
2. by
3. about
4. at
5. on

C

1. from
2. with
3. for
4. of
5. to

D

1. satisfied with
2. listened to
3. look it up
4. opposed to
5. ashamed of

내신 대비 실전문제 → pp. 144-147

선택형

1. ②	2. ⑤	3. ③	4. ④	5. ①
6. ④	7. ③	8. ⑤	9. ③	10. ①
11. ⑤	12. ①	13. ①	14. ④	15. ②
16. ④	17. ③	18. ②	19. ⑤	20. ③

서술형

21. nonetheless / however / still
22. (1) from, (2) in
23. for
24. ①, Please don't forget to take out the garbage.
25. but
26. (1) so, (2) and
27. in
28. Meanwhile

고난도 서술형

29. Karen's shoes were uncomfortable, so she took them off.
30. (1) However, (2) Moreover / Furthermore, (3) Consequently / As a result

선택형

1. rock and pop (락 음악과 팝 음악)
2. tiring과 really fun이 상반되는 의미이므로 그 사이에 but을 넣는 것이 맞다.
3. so는 결과를 나타내는데, ③에서 "해외에 가 본 적이 없다"는 것과 "3개 국어를 말한다"는 것이 원인-결과의 관계가 될 수 없다. But이 어울린다.
4. 문맥상 동시 상황을 나타내는 접속사 while이 가장 알맞다.
5. 쉼표 앞뒤에 있는 절이 상반된 내용을 담고 있기 때문에 이를 연결하는 데는 Though가 적합하다.
6. 첫 번째 빈칸에는 조건을 나타내는 접속사 If가 어울리고, 두 번째 빈칸에는 원인을 나타내는 접속사 as가 알맞다.
7. 접속사 since가 시간의 부사절을 이끌어 과거의 특정 시점 이후 계속되는 일을 나타낼 수 있다. 이때 주절에는 현재완료 시제를 쓴다. ③을 제외한 나머지 문장은 모두 이유를 나타낸다.
8. 빈칸에는 이유를 나타내는 접속사 Since, As, Because가 적합하고, 조건을 나타내는 접속사 If도 쓸 수 있다.
9. 첫 번째 빈칸에는 계절 앞에 쓰는 전치사 in, 두 번째 빈칸에는 "~안에"라는 장소의 전치사 in이 필요하다.
10. 부산에 관한 설명을 추가하는 내용이므로 접속부사 Furthermore가 알맞다.
11. 결과를 나타내는 접속부사가 필요한데 because는 이에 해당하지 않는다.
12. A는 서두를 필요가 없다는 의견인데, B는 곧 시작해야 한다는 의견이므로 빈칸에는 Still(그래도)이 적합하다.
13. 첫 번째 빈칸에는 작은 장소 앞에 쓰는 전치사 at, 두 번째 빈칸에는 특정 시각(midnight) 앞에 쓰는 전치사 at이 필요하다.
14. ④의 for는 동사 wait와 함께 "~을 기다리다"는 의미의 동사구를 이루고, 나머지는 모두 "~동안"이라는 의미의 시간을 나타낸다.
15. be similar to: "~와 유사하다"
    be amazed at: "~을 보고 놀라다"
16. 특정 기간을 나타내는 명사 앞에서 "~동안"이라는 의미를 나타낼 때는 during을 쓴다.
17. look for: "~을 찾다"
18. dream about: "~에 관해 꿈꾸다" 채널, 텔레비전, 인터넷 등 앞에는 전치사 on을 쓴다.
19. prepare for: "~을 준비하다"
20. 첫 번째 빈칸에는 "~가 …하는 것을 도와주다"는 의미의 관용적인 표현인 help someone with something에 쓰이는 with가 적합하고, 두 번째 빈칸에는 "~와 함께"라는 의미의 전치사 with가 알맞다.

서술형

21. 세미콜론(;) 앞뒤로 상반된 내용을 다루고 있기 때문에 빈칸에는 nonetheless / however가 알맞다.
22. 첫 번째 빈칸에는 "~로부터"라는 의미의 전치사 from, 두 번째 빈칸에는 be interested in (~에 관심이 있다)에 쓰이는 전치사 in이 알맞다.
23. 첫 번째 빈칸에는 이유를 나타내는 전치사 for, 두 번째 빈칸에는 be responsible for ("~에 책임이 있다")의 for가 필요하다.
24. take out the garbage: "쓰레기를 내놓다"
25. 바꾼 문장의 쉼표 앞뒤가 상반되는 내용이므로 빈칸에는 but이 알맞다.
26. 첫 번째 빈칸에는 결과를 나타내는 접속사 so, 두 번째 빈칸에는 연속적인 행위를 나열하고 있으므로 접속사 and가 필요하다.
27. 옷이나 장식품 앞에 전치사 in을 써서 "~을 착용한"이라는 의미를 나타낸다.
28. Meanwhile ("그 사이에")

고난도 서술형

29. 주어진 단어 가운데 이유를 나타내는 접속사가 없고 대신 결과를 나타내는 so가 보인다. 이를 기준으로 앞뒤에 원인과 결과를 나타내는 절을 배치한다. take off: "벗다"
30. 빈칸 (1)의 앞뒤에는 상반된 내용이 있기 때문에 빈칸에는 however가 적합하고, (2)의 앞뒤로는 동물들이 줄어든 이유를 나열하고 있으므로 (2)에는 Furthermore 또는 Moreover가 알맞다. (3) 뒤에는 이러한 현상의 결과를 서술하고 있으므로 (3)에는 Consequently 또는 As a result가 적합하다.

Quattro Grammar
Start

(주)컴퍼스미디어